SIX-STRING HEROES

PHOTOGRAPHS OF GREAT GUITARISTS

BY

NEIL ZLOZOWER

FOREWORD BY STEVE VAI

TEXT BY STEVEN ROSEN

CHRONICLE BOOKS

SAN FRANCISCO

Library of Congress Cataloging-in-Publication Data available.

ISBN: 978-0-8118-7027-6

Manufactured in China.

Art Direction & Design by Tom Jermann / t42design

10 9 8 7 6 5 4 3 2 1

Chronicle Books LLC
680 Second Street
San Francisco, CA 94107
www.chroniclebooks.com

Special thanks to

Zak "Mr. COOL" Zlozower (as always!!)

My parents, Hyman and Claire Zlozower

Tom Jermann and Toby Yoo of t42design
Steve Vai, THANKS for the GREAT idea for the book Bro!!!
Steve Mockus
Steve Rosen
Ruby
Commando

Baret Lepejian
Vic Lepejian
Rosa Gomez
And all the staff at A&I Photographic and Digital Services!!!

Dulcinea Circelli, thanks for everything baby!!!
Bill Lonero, thanks for the "special services"!!!!!
David Atlas, you are truly AMAZING!!!! THANKS!!!!!
Zakk and Barbaranne Wylde, LOVE YOU GUYS!!!!!
Slash
Peter Malick
Emmy Burns
Dr. Paul Freeman
Sandy Martin

Buddha
The Dalai Lama
Nyree Bird
Dick Caffey "Mr Norton"
Matt "Awake" Beal

And to all the great guitarists all over the world who
have given people countless hours of musical enjoyment,
THANKS!!!!!!!!!!!!!!!!!!!!!!!!!!!!!!!!

3

FOREWORD

Why the guitar? you ask.
Perhaps because it's the coolest instrument in the world.
Well, at least the people in this book think so.

For most of them, the first time they ever laid eyes on the instrument, its intoxicating allure was swift and explosive. Yet there was never a moment when they made the conscious choice to become a guitar player. Because that would mean there had been an option. For them, the calling of the guitar was irresistible.

Its graceful curves, its slender neck, its variety of shapes and colors, its infinity of sounds, and the way it feels against the body when slung over the shoulder and gripped in the hands are like Cupid's arrows piercing the hearts of its lovers.

Once they experienced its enticing charms, they knew they could never keep their hands off. They realized their six-string journey of discovery would have no end. It's a magnificent life sentence.

When you're in high school, there's nothing cooler than playing guitar in a rock band. It doesn't matter if you're rich, poor, short, fat, cute, or ugly, you are just fuckin' cool, baby, because you play guitar in a rock band. And one of the coolest things is the connection that forms among band members. It's a bond unlike any other.

Going through first-time life experiences, such as driving a car, having sex, breaking up, making up, and getting drunk or high, are richer experiences when you voyage through them with your band brothers.

Once they left behind the passion and warfare of their adolescent years, the people in the pages of this book variously faced challenges of addiction, rising to fame, attaining material success, reveling in excess, enduring financial ruin, hitting bottom, making comebacks, finding God, and experiencing touring demands that could cripple a platoon of Navy SEALs. Through it all, their guitar has been a faithful friend that is always there to turn to.

It offers unconditional acceptance to everyone, regardless of race, gender, religion, or personal shortcomings. It is a companion you can communicate with anytime, and it will never judge or abandon you.

With our hands on the guitar and a willingness to explore our innermost being, the instrument becomes a conduit of self-expression to the outside. What lies underneath the skin comes to the surface. The cool become cooler, the geeky become geekier, the strong turn mighty, and the superficial hopelessly devolve. We cannot hide who we really are. We are naked to the world.

The guitar moves with us physically and emotionally, with a voice that bends, whispers, screams, purrs, and moans. And it does these things differently from any other instrument, provided that the player is a capable seducer.

The guitar breathes fire into all the styles of music that it plays. Just look at the expanse of its playground—jazz, classical, blues, folk, country, and, of course, rock. What a vapid world we would live in without it . . . quiet, too. Not only does it rule the world of its players, but entire subcultures also can be generated by the various ongoing permutations in guitar design. This is evidenced by the resurgent metal scene at the turn of the 21st century, spawned by the tuned-down seven-string guitar.

Some people devotedly practice their guitar for 15 hours a day and become shred machines, and some never practice and can barely form an E Major chord. Some people play a note or two, then polish their guitar and hang it on the wall like it's a museum piece, while others smash it into little pieces and set it on fire. But regardless of all that, what moves the listener is the sincerity and confidence of the player.

A *true* guitar hero enters a guitar-induced hypnotic state and immerses the audience in an ocean of trance-induced audio elixir, thus revealing the secrets of his soul.

I have found that most great guitar players never feel as though they are good enough. A sign of humility, it is also a sign of real greatness.

Because of the technical advantages of its design, the dynamic range of the guitar is gigantic. There's no limit to how softly and tenderly it can be caressed, or to how fiercely and chaotically it can be wailed upon. If you think about it, every note ever played on any guitar has never been played exactly the same way twice. Perhaps there are as many guitar notes that have been plucked as there are snowflakes that have fallen on the Earth. And you could probably find half of them in one of my solos . . . the stormy, icy ones.

Whether its sound is harshly distorted, crystal clean, organically acoustic, or highly processed, the instrument's most enchanting attraction is the way its vibrating strings create attunement deep within its admirers. This resonance is uniquely satisfying, and to go without it for any period of time can result in auditory withdrawal pangs. We need our daily dose of strings!

Now it's time to get esoteric on your ass.

I see the universe as a series of infinite vibrations that are resonating within each other. From the motions of the tiny atom to the orbits of the solar system to the expansion of the cosmos —all is in a state of constant vibration. Each color of the rainbow vibrates at its own frequency, and though they are more refined, thoughts and feelings are a form of vibration existing within a subtler dimension. All are set into motion by a primal action. And what that is, God only knows.

I believe that no other instrument captures the vibrational microcosm of the Creation like the guitar. Every "kirchang" of its strings is like the creation of a universe set into motion by its "kirchanger." Aha! Perhaps that's why so many guitarists have a God complex . . . ?

Nah, c'mon, we all know that lead singers are the real creators of the universe, for fuck's sake!

Playing the guitar is a cathartic expression of self-discovery. And here's the good news. You don't have to be one of the people in this book to play it. Anyone can play guitar, and maybe everyone should. Please hear this loud and clear: It's your right to play it, and it does not matter how good or bad you are. Guitar playing is a form of artistic expression and freedom, and in reality, there's no wrong way to do it. Even if you have the technique or strength to set only one note into motion, it can envelop your spirit and light up your world. Just try it!

If you happen to be one of the elite players who made it into this book, it means that you have heard the call of the guitar, fallen in love with it, and have taken your life's journey with a handful of six-string soul. It was also inevitable that at some point along the way, your destiny dictated you would be given orders by a more powerful voice than that of your own muse. It was the voice of the infamous creator of the photos in this book.

The voice that demands, "Chin up! Come on, get your fuckin' chin up and give me some fuckin' attitude! WE AIN'T GOT ALL FUCKIN' DAY!"

Such are the demands of Neil Zlozower.

Now, the music industry has its share of colorful and talented people, and many of them are in front of the camera. Although Zlozower is one of the people on the other side of the camera, he's no less gifted at what he does than the people whose historical images he preserves for posterity. He's a character such as you will never find anywhere else. I'll try to give you a clue as to the intensity that is "The Zloz."

Neil Zlozower is rock and roll to the bone! For 40 years, he's been nailing on film images of renowned "kirchangers," and this book is the culmination of that passion.

Zlozower is brutally honest. There's no stop valve between his brain and his mouth. He doesn't care who you are or how famous you are; if you are talking to him, you'd better be prepared to hear the Zloz truth. Whenever I'm with him, I can't wait to hear what's going to come out of his mouth next. He's freakin' hilarious! I've heard him say things that were so raunchy that the input jack on my guitar closed up.

He's loud and raw. Just read his intro to this book and check out how many exclamation marks he uses. He's yelling at you, even when you can't hear him.

He's ferociously protective of his work and has set precedents around the world for the rights of photographers. There is a copyright notice somewhere in this book regarding the use of these photos. I suggest adhering to it.

But more than anything, he is a conscientious professional who is attentive to every detail and does whatever it takes to get the shot. The guy is always on time and tireless when he works. He still gets excited over a good idea and is not afraid to try to execute it. I've seen him clamber through some of Hollywood's filthiest alleys in the blazing L.A. heat, naked from the waist up, wearing nothing but a tattoo of the Dalai Lama on one arm, a tattoo of the Buddha on the other, torn-up motorcycle boots, and funky gray shorts so skimpy that his sweaty balls are hanging out, just to snag the ideal photo.

There's a rough charm about him, but you have to have the right lens to view it. Underneath the wildman in the shorts is a person who is deeply respectful of those he works with. He's not content until his subjects are also happy with his shots.

Neil is arguably the finest rock photographer in history, and this book is one of his masterpieces.

But I have to end now, because I just got an e-mail from him that says, "Are you fucking finished writing yet?!?!?!?!?!?!?!?!?!?! Come on, Stevie darling, I AIN'T GOT ALL FUCKIN' DAY!!"

Hey, Zloz, keep your balls in your shorts. I'm done.

— Steve Vai

INTRODUCTION

Guitarists and guitars, wow, where do I start!? When the Beatles played on *Ed Sullivan* in 1964, I think it opened the world's (and my) ears to real rock and roll music as never before, but it really wasn't very guitar-oriented. It was when I first heard Cream and Jimi Hendrix that I really got into the guitar as an instrument. They really opened my eyes to what the guitar is capable of, ESPECIALLY when I got to see them both play LIVE, at 13 and 14 years old!!!! Obviously, there were talented players before Jimi and Eric, but they took the instrument to new heights, and probably influenced a lot of kids to abandon their original "goals in life" and become rock guitar players!!

Cream was definitely a unique band by the standards of the day. Jack Bruce (bass god, vocalist d'elegance, and amazing harp player), Ginger Baker (my favorite all-time drummer) and guitarist extraordinaire, ERIC CLAPTION. Eric had been in the Yardbirds and John Mayall's Bluesbreakers, and was already a very well respected guitarist at that time. He was the first guitarist that I remember using the wah-wah pedal, which at 13 years old I thought was PRETTY COOL. Cream was my first concert ever, on February 23, 1968, at the Santa Monica Civic Auditorium. I still remember it like it was yesterday: with the curtain still closed, the announcer said, "AND NOW, CREAM!" and Clapton started playing wah-wah on the beginning of "Tales of Brave Ulysses," then the curtain OPENS and they BLAZE into the song. It's hard to describe the lasting impression that night left on this 13-year-old kid!!

I never photographed Jimi, but I was fortunate to see him four times. The first time I saw him was at the Hollywood Bowl in February 1968, and it was truly an EXPERIENCE!!! The next few times I saw him I was too musically immature to really understand what he was trying to do, and I remember walking away from those shows thinking, "that wasn't so great," but later when I looked back, I realized how brilliant and advanced he really was. His death was a tragic loss, and he's one of my true idols.

I've been shooting photos in the music industry for 40 years and have been fortunate to have been able to photograph, and hang with, some of the greatest guitarists that ever graced this planet. My "job" isn't always fun and games, as most people imagine it, but whether I'm shooting at my studio in Hollywood, California, or at a live gig in front of 50,000 screaming, maniacal fans, I must have done something really spectacular in a previous lifetime to be able to come back and be given the occupation that I now have!!! Truly a "once in a lifetime" journey!!!!

I'd like to take this space to give a little insight into the guitar players who have inspired me and brought me hours of happiness by listening to their music and personally knowing and working with them. Here goes . . .

For all-out brutality, aggressiveness, attack, timing, and sickness (good for me!!) NO ONE beats Ritchie Blackmore!!! I've seen him many, many times with Deep Purple and Rainbow, and his guitar playing and live performances always amaze and fascinate me.

When I was younger and saw Led Zeppelin in concert, I was really astonished by Jimmy's playing the guitar with a violin bow on "Dazed and Confused." Up until Zeppelin would play that song, I would keep thinking, "When is Jimmy going to use the bow? When is Jimmy going to use the bow?" And when he did, I would LOSE MY MIND!!! No one did that, and I thought it was the coolest thing in the world. Simply breathtaking!!! Jimmy is a true innovator.

If someone asked me, "Zloz, who do you like to see live more than anyone else?" I would probably say ERIC SARDINAS!! I've seen almost everyone in this book in their prime, but I still never get tired of seeing Eric play. He's a great vocalist, and an amazing entertainer, and his guitar playing talents are too unique to describe!!! His records are good, but don't do JUSTICE to his live performances!!! If you want to be entertained, go see Eric Sardinas in concert!!

I know, I know, she's a girl, BUT don't underestimate her: Allison Robertson is a great guitarist. I never really liked any "girl bands" until I heard the Donnas, and Allison plays all the hot licks in that band (she's also in the Chelsea Girls). She's like the female Angus Young!! She gets a great sound from her Gibson, and she plays way better than some of the other so-called guitar heroes out there. PLUS she definitely looks hotter than all of them!!!!

Rory Gallagher isn't a household name when it comes to guitarists, but he ranks at the very, very top of my GUITAR GODS list. I must have seen Rory 30 times live, and he never failed to ignite a fire in me and everyone else in the audience at his shows. Like Eric Sardinas, his albums never really captured the raw energy of his live performances, but nevertheless he wrote brilliant songs, and played incredible electric, slide, and acoustic guitar. He was one of those performers that gave 200 percent every night, and every live performance was different from night to night. He was even asked to join the Rolling Stones when Brian Jones died, before Mick Taylor joined, but he turned it down!!! I still listen to Rory probably three times a week, if not more. Every guitar aficionado should have Rory's *Irish Tour, 1974* in their record collection—it's a MUST HAVE!!! If you don't love that album, go check yourself into a mental institution, PERIOD!!!!

Edward Van Halen single-handedly changed the face of guitar playing FOREVER!!! NO ONE played the guitar like Edward did before him!! Many tried to imitate his style, but no one could really play like Ed does. I was EXTREMELY fortunate to be able to work with Ed and Van Halen from 1978 to 1984 and witness his talents in the recording studio, backstage warming up, and onstage shredding live. I remember there would be nights when I would be shooting in the photo pit and I would be watching Ed's hands move and playing and I would just put down my camera and stare at him in AMAZEMENT!!!! I NEVER saw anyone do things with the guitar like Ed did. He was and is a genius, and continues to set standards that no one else can match.

I met Slash in 1983, way before he was in Guns N' Roses. I remember the first photo session in my studio with the band, but it was way different than the usual sessions I was doing in that period with bands like Mötley, RATT, and Poison. The first time I heard *Appetite for Destruction* I knew they were going to explode. Slash is what I call a "feeling" guitar player. He can play the same song, 365 nights a year, and each night he will play it slightly differently, depending on how he feels and the circumstances that night, but it ALWAYS sounds GREAT!!!! Besides being an amazing guitarist, he is one of the nicest human beings I have ever met and worked with. I love the guy!!!

George Thorogood: You either hate him or you love him, BUT I LOVE HIM!!!!

Quiet Riot was trying as hard as hell to get a record deal in the late '70s. They had this skinny young kid on guitar who everybody was raving about named Randy Rhoads. I did some work with the band and saw them live a few times, but couldn't understand why people were raving about Randy's playing until I saw him at an Ozzy rehearsal in Hollywood in 1981. This was a NEW Randy, just fucking blazing on his guitar—I was like HOLY SHIT, what happened to Randy!? He must have locked himself up in his bedroom 24-7 for four years, because what I saw was unbelievable!!! Randy was ALWAYS practicing; you would be talking with him and he would have a guitar around his neck, and his fingers would be playing a million miles a second while he was looking directly at you, holding up his end of the conversation. He was a sweet, quiet, shy, soft-spoken person who was taken away from the world far too soon, and his death was another tragic loss.

Sometime around 1984, a friend called me and said, "Hey, wanna go with me to Long Beach to see Alcatrazz play?" My response was, "Why? Yngwie's not in the band anymore." They had some new kid named Steve Vai, who I figured couldn't be as good as Yngwie. BOY WAS I WRONG!!! I wouldn't really

become aware of Steve's talents as a guitar player till I saw him with the David Lee Roth band during the "Eat Them and Smile" tour in 1986. I was used to hearing Ed play with Dave, but Steve brought in a whole new breath of fresh air, and coupled with the bass-playing talents of Billy Sheehan and the drumming of Greg Bissonette, the band was unstoppable. It was like a TSUNAMI hitting you right in your face!!!! I have worked with Steve for 23 years now, and I have to say that Steve (to me) is probably the most versatile guitar player I have ever heard. He can do things with the guitar that no one else can, and I've been lucky enough to see him do it all!!!!! And just like Slash, he's one of the nicest, most PROFESSIONAL artists I have ever met and worked with. (And thanks for the great intro to the book!!!)

I saved the best for last. ZAKK WYLDE!!! I've known Zakk since he started playing for Ozzy in 1987, and our working and personal relationship has grown throughout the years. Zakk calls me "Father Zloz"!!! He is truly a one-of-a-kind human being, and I love him and his family dearly. His words are always from his heart, and he calls it as he sees it. As far as his guitar playing goes, a word of caution: DON'T GET IN ITS WAY 'cause it will devastate you, annihilate you, destroy you, shred you, ream you a new asshole, and chew you up and spit you out!!! It's fucking BRUTAL!!!! I love it!!!!!!

— Neil Zlozower

ZAKK WYLDE AND NEIL ZLOZOWER | 2006

JIMMY PAGE | 1975

JIMMY PAGE | 1975

"My vocation is more in composition really than in anything else. Building up harmonies. Using the guitar, orchestrating the guitar like an army—a guitar army. I think that's where it's at, really, for me. I'm talking about actual orchestration in the same way you'd orchestrate a classical piece of music. Instead of using brass and violins, you treat the guitars with synthesizers or other devices; give them different treatments so that they have enough frequency range and scope and everything to keep the listener as totally committed to it as the player is. It's a difficult project, but it's one that I've got to do."

———————————

"I've got two different approaches, like a schizophrenic guitarist, really. I mean, onstage is totally different than the way that I approach it in the studio."

———————————

"I don't practice. It's usually the acoustic guitar for a start and it's usually in a tuning. I sort of change tunings around a bit and I'm searching for new chords and shapes and things. I don't just sit down and play scales and things. I should have done but I never did. I can't play a scale. You think I'm kidding but I'm not. I can't. Well I can, I can play the notes, but it's true, though, I can't play a barre chord. It's true. It's unbelievable, isn't it? It's true though. It's just try to do whatever you can do on an instrument and give it 100 percent of what you can do with the time you have to do it. I push myself as far as I can go within the instrument at that point in time."

Jimmy Page 1977

12

"The guitar is an emotional thing, and you play it consciously; you consciously mark out the notes and squeeze the string, but there's a sort of unconscious thing there too. And the emotion comes from that; there are things going into there where you almost don't realize you're putting in. And I wanted the orchestra behind every one of those parts; it had to have that tension in it and that emotion in it. So I didn't want someone doing that on a keyboard. Synthesizers were already beginning to be around and I didn't want synthesizers, which at that time were very cold."

"Hendrix was my biggest idol. I saw him in the very early days when he was supporting the Who and everyone was sort of skeptical, and I didn't want to think he was that good and I was so knocked out I couldn't believe it. I never really copied him, but the style and the feel influenced me a lot. I think he made the guitar something better than it was before he came along. He was using just one Marshall stack, which was pretty ordinary, and a Stratocaster, and The Who at that time were using like four stacks each. And I saw him with the Move and they had four Marshall stacks each. And Hendrix came on and just blew them totally away."

Brian May 1983

15

16

BRIAN MAY | 1976 | 1977

JOE SATRIANI | 1997

"I try to push my own limits. The only fun is to go in the studio thinking, 'I don't know if I can do this but if I pull it off, it's going to make me feel really great.'"

"My first guitar lessons lasted two weeks and it was 'Jingle Bells.' It didn't make any sense at all. I wanted to know how to play like Hendrix and Jimmy Page and sound like Jethro Tull records. All three of those were very big on composition. Like 'Third Stone from the Sun' right alongside 'Foxy Lady' and the *Stand Up* album by Jethro Tull. As a kid growing up on Long Island, I had no idea where Ian Anderson was getting that from."

"I could make a big list of everything I can't play and everything I'm struggling with. I'm grateful that people don't notice that. I've never felt like the guitar players who could play everything. When I get something I think is interesting, I work on it for years. With my music, there's no room for spacing out and just playing what fits."

Joe Satriani 1989

22

24

"I didn't particularly want to play the guitar; I just fell in love with it after I got involved with it. I wanted to play the saxophone originally but I couldn't afford one at the time."

"My speed is not a deliberate thing. I became interested in listening to horn players, saxophone players, just the vibe that they created. They seemed to be able to create a thing where you'd hear a lot of notes, but they wouldn't be a stream of notes. I'd hear it like a pattern. I suppose everybody's got things that they do because it's like a personality thing. I've been working hard with scales, but it's endless; I like mixing them up. I just let my ears judge what's right or what's not."

Allan Holdsworth 1978

"I'm still the same idiot I've always been. I'm a little wiser; I make my decisions more astutely. But at the same time, I'm still very playful and I'm still trying to discover new shit. I still care about the guitar, still care about music. At this point, I care a lot less about trying to keep up with the Joneses. I mean, when you look at the Top 40 market, what's selling and what's not and to stay in the music business, I took the road to be a little more artistic."

Steve Lukather 1989

26

MICK RALPHS | 1977

RONNIE MONTROSE | 1976

"One thing I can say about a solo, and how to play one, is to make it like breathing. If you're going to play lead, sing it out first; then you'll know if it's going to be effective or not. If you start singing the line and have to gasp for breath, you've over-extended yourself. Make your solos as vocally oriented as possible, just as if someone were singing it. So the sound grows more human and natural."

"When I first started playing, I wanted to be the best guitar player in the world—but then I came to realize it was a big world! That was a pretty wide goal, and there is no best guitar player. I just wanted to be as expressive as I could with what I did, and reach as many people as possible. I wanted to be a sincere guitarist. Now, the goal I've set for myself—of course I'm always trying to be a better fingerpicker and acoustic player—is to be as sincere with the notes as possible, so that what I'm playing is what I really mean. It sounds kind of corny, but that's the way I feel."

Ronnie Montrose circa 1977

"When Eric Clapton came out with the Bluesbreakers record, that's when I decided if I wanted my own style, I had to go another direction. Because it was too seductive. I wanted to play like that like crazy, but so did everybody else. I'll steal a few licks, but I'm not going to go that way. It was about '65 or '66. I was in a band called the Preachers before the Herd and we did a lot of jazz, whether I liked it or not. The bandleader said, 'Take these albums . . . it's Friday night, we rehearse Monday, learn them.' There was everything from Wes Montgomery, George Benson with Jack McDuff, Joe Pass, Charlie Christian, and after studying it for a while I realized that I really enjoyed it. But I loved the blues as well. . . . Now I've got this melodic thing combined with the jazz influence and then the blues and R&B, and Steve Cropper is in there somewhere as well. My objective was for someone to listen to a few notes and go, 'That's Peter Frampton.' My style completely evolved during Humble Pie, and the *Rockin' the Fillmore* album is the best example of me sort of just realizing I've got this almost recognizable style."

Peter Frampton 2003

"Mick Taylor had this beauty, you know? I put him in the category of Peter Green—right up there with Peter Green. I mean, unbelievable. I loved Paul Kossoff. I used to go into Selmers in Charing Cross Road and Paul would sell me my strings. I was in the Herd and he was, 'Hey man, it's so cool to meet you, man!' Not knowing that he was gonna do what he did, you know? I was a huge fan of that vibrato. It's such a cool vibrato; it's so unique and no one can do it like he did."

Peter Frampton 2008

30

PETER FRAMPTON | 1977

32

"From a starting point to an ending point, there really is no one certain thing that I do in a solo; it just comes as it feels as a natural thing. And that's basically the way I do all my lead work. My lead work is straight from the heart to the fingers."

Ricky Medlocke 1980

"The main slide player I listened to was Hound Dog Taylor. He really set me straight. And Elmore James. There was a period of time when everything was Robert Johnson. And then when I started fooling around with the electric guitar, everything was Elmore James. Actually, the way I got started playing slide was in San Francisco; I used to play on street corners to make money, with my guitar case open. And the slide was the loudest and it got people to notice. I used to play all day long. I didn't sing, just played. After a while, I got pretty good at it."

"When I solo, it's not in the vein of someone like Ted Nugent, Eric Clapton, Jimi Hendrix. My guitar playing is basically derived from acoustic playing. Which is not unlike Elmore James or Muddy Waters, because that's how they started. I'm kind of right in gear with them. Soloing is not my thing; I can take a solo but I'm not a lead guitarist."

George Thorogood 1978

GEORGE THOROGOOD | 2007

34

TOM SCHOLZ | 1978 ~ ALEX LIFESON | 1977

FRANK MARINO | 1978 ~ STEVE MILLER | 1976

"The balance between being a lead instrument and being in touch with the rhythm section. I think that it has gone through three different stages, and this is the beginning of the third stage. I know, for myself, my soloing has gone from trying to play as fast as I can and trying to play as bizarre a solo as I can to more of a rhythm, chordal type thing. I think that's more of the direction generally for the future and for myself certainly."

"I think when I sit down to do solos, a sound can be inspiring. It may not necessarily be correct for that solo or that song, but a sound can be inspiring. I think that's what you mean: Can a sound inspire you to do something? I think that's really the first step. You can't do a solo for a song that's calling for a bluesy, sad type solo and use a really dry, thin guitar sound. So you start putting on interesting echoes and reverb in the background. You make it so that you play one note, and that one note just goes, 'Oh!' Tears come to your eyes."

Alex Lifeson 1984

"You've got to use everything you can, everything you can get, but use it wisely. You gotta use your tremolo arm, your wah-wah, your boxes; you've gotta use everything if you're going to be an electric guitar player. My concept of electric guitar playing is taking a sound that's in my head. Some people say it comes out like a woodwind, but in my head it comes out as electricity and it's gotta be done through electricity. When you utilize that harnessed energy and you use it to actually create impressions of things you're thinking about or things you're feeling or things that you want people to feel or think about, then you're truly an electric guitarist."

"I don't think. If I'm thinking at all when I'm playing, I'm not playing. As soon as I start thinking, I start fucking up. That's the hardest thing to do."

Frank Marino 1978

"I spent three years in an echo chamber playing huge chords after I saw Cream. I just loved it. They played 14 nights at the Fillmore and I went and it was just unbelievable. I was just so jealous, walking around the Fillmore hating those guys for doing everything I ever thought in my wildest dreams I'd like to do on the guitar. When I heard Fresh Cream it broke my heart. It took me a real long time, about 10 days of walking around the Fillmore and badmouthing them and everything, and they were just playing incredibly, and then I finally got over it and went, 'God, he's really great.'"

Steve Miller 1984

36

PAT TRAVERS | 1978

JOE STRUMMER | 1983

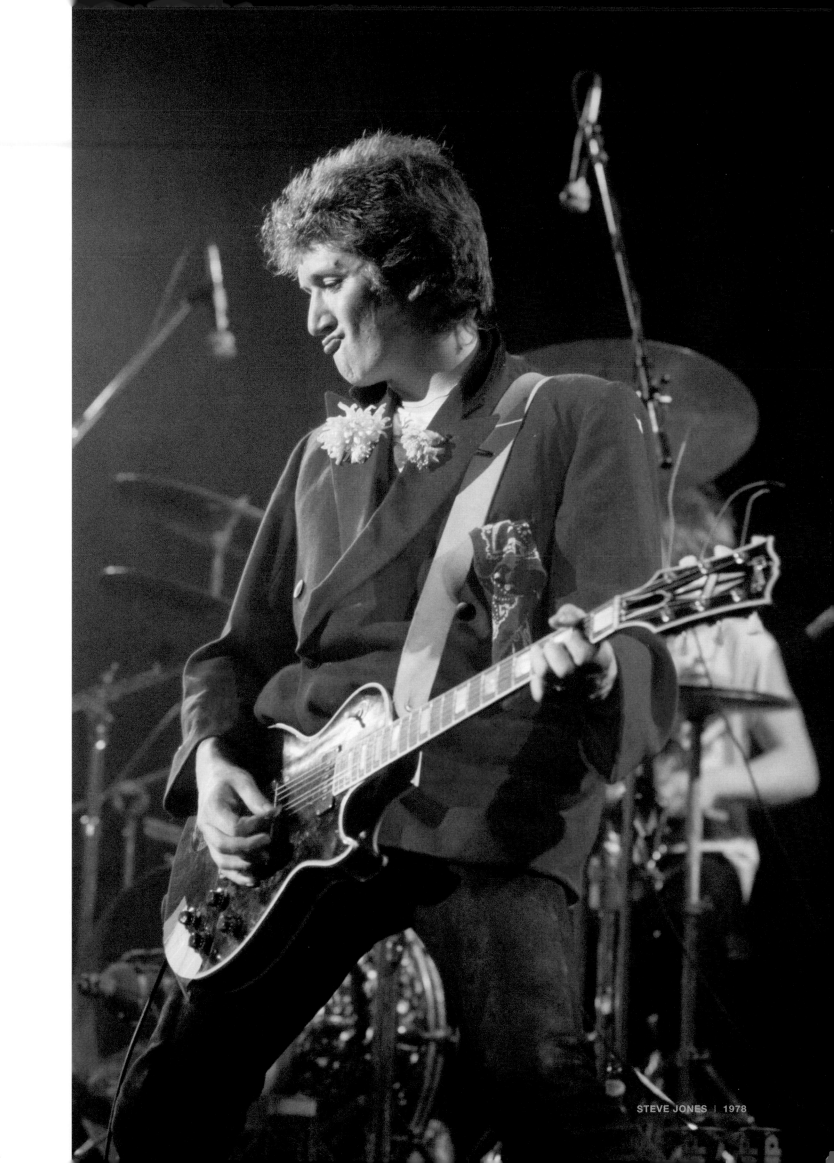

STEVE JONES | 1978

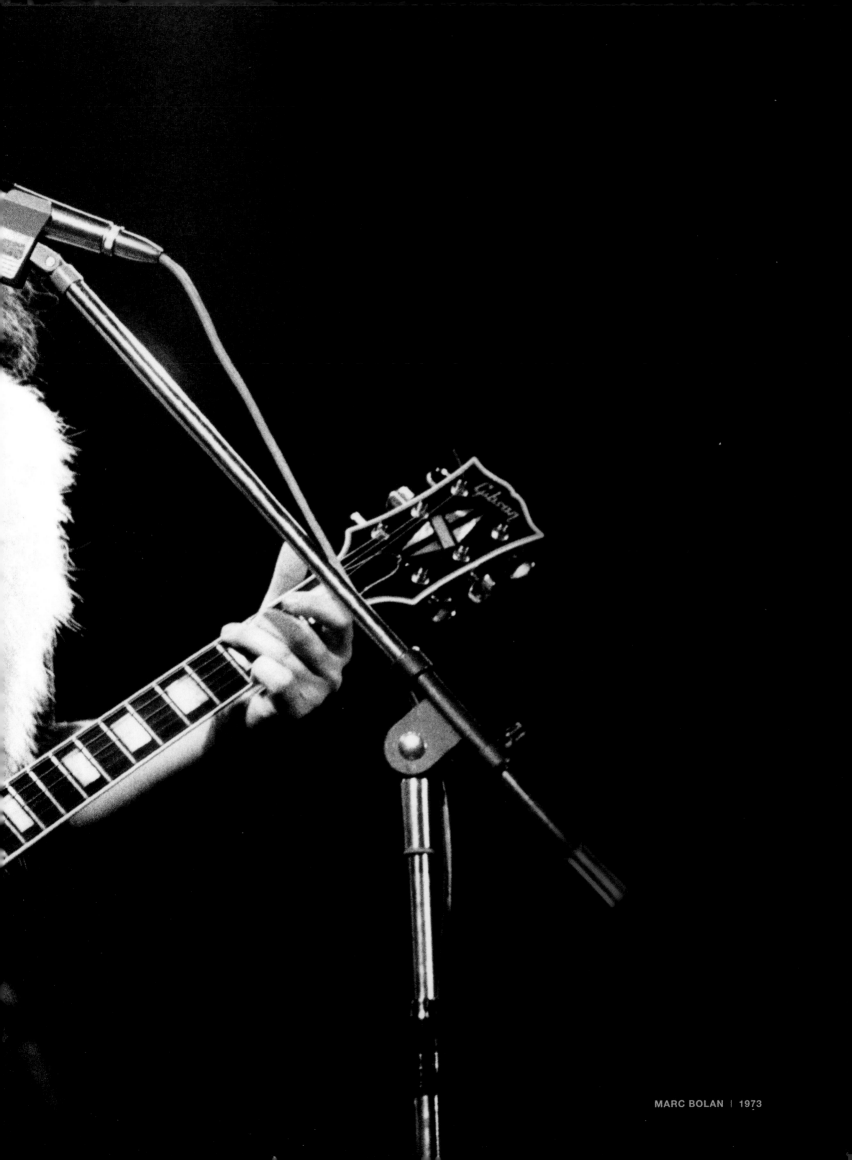

MARC BOLAN | 1973

"Guys like Johnny Lang are a breath of fresh air because he really cares, he's really celebrating the soul of man. Guys like him and Kenny Wayne Shepherd. And listening to Buddy Guy and the experimental maneuvers of Steve Vai and Joe Satriani."

Ted Nugent 2001

"Every time I pick up the guitar, jeez, these cool guitar licks come firing out of my hands because I can't wait to do it because it's so fresh and raw again. Because I just got done gutting a moose or something!"

"Here's Ted Nugent in a nutshell: I fuckin' love it! I love the fuckin' licks, I love the energy and the electricity of what the guitar provides me. I'm 60-motherfucking years old and I love it more now than when I first got that electric guitar and plugged into that little Magnavox amplifier and started making noises."

Ted Nugent 2008

"I suppose everybody was impacted by Hendrix. But you couldn't tell by listening to me! I'm an entertainer and a songwriter and I get to play guitar once in a while. I'm a good rhythm player. I can play the lead stuff and I can play the fast stuff and I can do all the hammering things."

44

"I've learned stuff from some of the people I've played with like John McCurry and Brad Gillis and Eddie Van Halen. I'd meet all these different guys and they'd say, 'Here, Rick, try this.' And I just look at 'em and go, 'No, if I need that I'll call you.'"

Rick Nielson 1986

46

ANDY SUMMERS | 1981

48

THE EDGE | 1983

"It's not so much what you got guitar-wise, it's what you do with what you got. You've got to sort of have an idea and then it's pretty easy to find a guitar to get to what you hear in your head. I guess."

Lindsey Buckingham 2008

"The most fun I have is when I'm doing leads. I definitely don't focus as much time on it as I initially did because I focus more on the songs. I don't sit down every day and play four or five hours a day. In the old days when I was in the Tygers—I'm definitely better than that. These days, instead of getting frantic about it, I'll just push 'record' and play. I think it's more relaxed now. More so than singing; where I can really let myself go is the guitar."

"The guitar role in the Police has taken a direction for a purpose. In terms of the role of the guitar and the Police as a three-piece group, our philosophy musically has always been to try and make it something new. To change the idea of a three-piece group and to have all the instruments so it's like three soloists playing all the time. So the guitar part is like a solo all the time and so are the drums and the bass. I think that Cream in a way were also three soloists playing together, but they started playing a certain way, and everybody copied them for 10 years after . . . so we had to not do that."

"When I was a teenage guitar player, something that was a big thing for me was these three albums by Barney Kessel called *The Poll Winner's Trio*, which was Barney Kessel, Ray Brown, and Shelly Manne. I tried to copy those things and play them with a trio as a kid, and that ultimate expression finally came in the Police, which was a much more expanded version of that sort of thing."

Andy Summers 1989

"I respect Andy Summers and I really enjoy his guitar playing because he is a guitarist in a band. He's not a guitarist on his own; he's not 'the guitar player.' He's the guitarist in the band, and the band is the unit. It's one musical entity, and he's a part of it. I think that's really important. I think adding all the keyboards and synthesizers and stuff with us, it taught me that. It's not important to stand out; it's more important to be a piece of the whole pie. Yeah, the guitar hero doesn't jive with me."

Alex Lifeson 1984

"I'd get annoyed and pick the guitar up and smash it. At first people didn't realize how hard it was to learn to play like that. It involved a lot of determination and a lot of hard work and practice. It's just something I'll have to try and overcome. The accident happened over eight years ago, way before Sabbath or Tull. And when I joined Jethro they even said, 'What are those things on your fingers?' When I told them, they were quite surprised to find I could play guitar with these. I've had to adopt a totally different way of playing because of these fingers. I mean, it's much easier when the flesh is there as it should be. Instead of, say, pulling a note, I have to sort of push it up to get a vibrato. These tips are a bit clumsy and they slow me down and get in the way. I even have to wear leather on them to grip the strings."

Tony Iommi circa mid-1980s

"The music was very misinterpreted in the early years. The guitar sound was just something that came out of me that was totally different because it was like doomy and the riffs were a bit frightening. And you know, it was something that I felt. It's really a mystical thing. I was always trying to improve the guitar sound all the time and for many years I worked on that."

Tony Iommi 1995

52

"Half of my style is my attitude. What I lack in technique, I make up for in attitude. Hell, I've been working on the way I stand for years."

"There aren't too many rhythm players out there. Playing solos is just another way to disguise rhythm. Solos are another flavor. Some soloists use the rhythm as the vehicle and let the solo take you away. But for me, it's the rhythm that does it and then you put the solos on as icing on the cake. But all the pyrotechnics and the flash get all the press."

"I suppose if I wanted to be a guitar hero, I would have practiced more. I would have practiced scales and stuff. I like some amount of flash but I find it's not as important to me as some other things. I appreciate all those people out there, but a lot of it just washes over me. Only a few rise to the top, just like in any era."

Joe Perry 1987

54

55

"The wave of blues that we enjoyed, not only being a part of but influenced by, was ushered in by the English guys: The Stones, Clapton, Beck . . . which is kind of what got us to thinking, 'Hey, we can hot-rod this stuff and make it really fun to play for ZZ Top.'"

"Man, I hope when they're scattering my ashes over south Texas and they open the window in the airplane, they say, 'Here was a guy that liked the guitar.' That's all I can say; that would be all right by me. If that can be remembered, terrific."

Billy Gibbons 1986

"I love Billy Gibbons as a lead guitar player because he's a stylist; when that guy comes on, I know who that is. And that's not always so easy to do. He's got a lot of taste and flavor in what he does. I don't know that I've ever really kind of learned his licks or anything like that, but I appreciate him as a guitar player."

Tom Morello 2005

"I guess all my stuff comes from madness. I don't think there's enough experimentation going on, especially in the mainstream of music. There's not a lot of people willing to take many risks."

Tom Petty 1985

TOM PETTY | 1980

RICK DERRINGER | 1971 ~ "LONESOME" DAVE PEVERETT | 1973

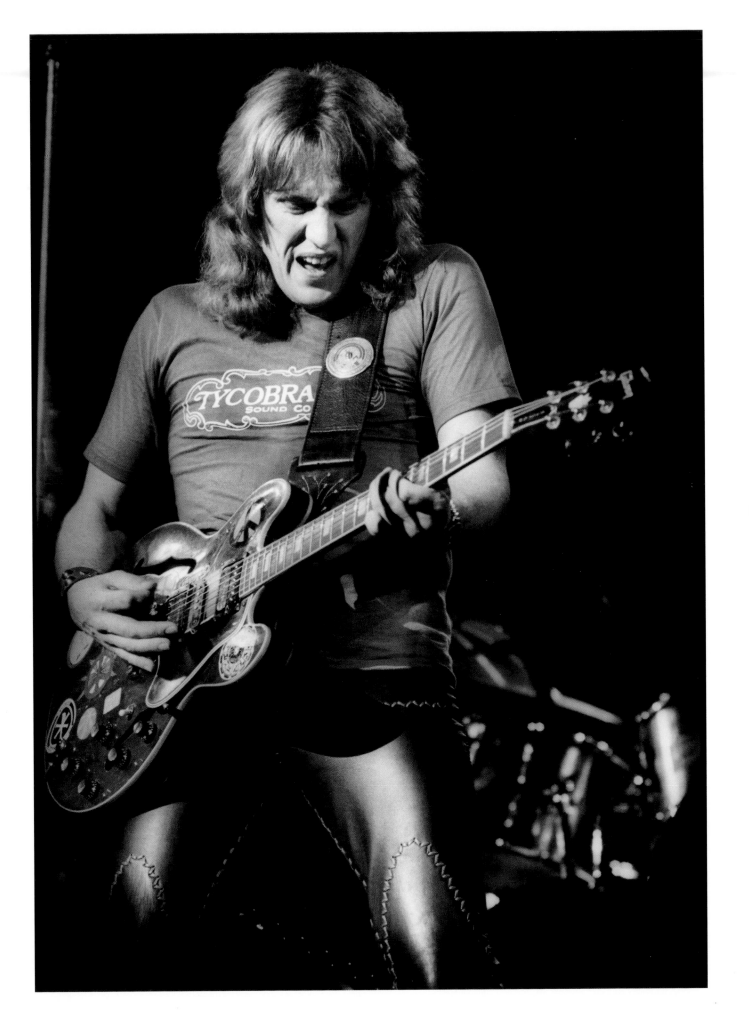

ALVIN LEE | 1974

"Most of the guitarists I like, but I try not to fashion myself on them. I might borrow a feel from them but I never actually sit down and try and copy anything. Even a guitarist who has been playing three months, I can sit down and learn something from him because often they don't have the limitations that I have. I just think in phrases and my hands fall in patterns; it's very difficult for me to kind of think of a new line."

Alvin Lee 1973

"Play your ass off all the time; play in front of people and experiment. Go back and listen to all those guitarists, the Yardbirds, James Burton with Ricky Nelson, Albert King. Learn all their licks, find out where they learned them. You got to start at the beginning; get your left hand doing what your brain wants it to, and then after a couple years you'll get that. Once you get the technical end down, express yourself, teach yourself. It's a long, hard trip, but if somebody starts and does what I say, maybe in two or three years he'll play some hot licks. And I hope they do because then I can copy them!"

Joe Walsh 1975

DICKIE BETTS | 1975

JOE WALSH | 1975

62

TOMMY SHAW AND JAMES YOUNG | 1978

"I try to hear in my head what color the song should be. Whether it should be crankin' or a little more subtle. I tried to always make it like that even if I had to construct a solo. It's easy enough to learn it after you've finished it, but to play it great as you're making it up, that's never really been my strong suit."

"J.Y. was strictly a rock and roll player, and I really tried to get some of his rock and roll moves. And J.Y. over the years picked up some of my more melodic things. My solos are melodies. You play whatever comes out and that seems to be what I'm inspired to play. I never really listened to any one particular player."

Tommy Shaw 1984

"I've never had any respect really for the guitar. I respected guitar players, of course, you know, and I understand their need for a good instrument, but for years and years and years, I didn't care what the guitar was like."

"It seemed mad for me to even try to compete with the likes of Beck and Clapton and Jimmy Page and people like that. I first saw Jimmy Page when he was 14 or 15, and he was already in a professional band. One year older than me, he was in a professional band at 16, and he was earning 30 pounds a week when I was just still in school. Playing like really fast stuff, and Ritchie Blackmore was in a jazz band—not a jazz band, he was in a kind of heavy pop rock, the Fleawreckers, or something like that. Some kind of Ventures-type outfit. You just listened to records like that open-mouthed at the time, and there was no question of being able to play that stuff."

Pete Townshend 1978

PETE TOWNSHEND | 1970

"I started to get quite interested in feedback, but I was very frustrated at first. I mean, there were a lot of brilliant young players around. Beck was around when he was in a group called the Triads or the Tridents or something. And Clapton was around, and various other people who could really play. And I was very frustrated because I couldn't do all that flash stuff. And so I just started to get into feedback and expressing myself physically. And it just led to one day, I was banging around on my guitar, making noises, banging it on the ceiling in this club, and the neck broke off. And everybody started to laugh. They're all kinda going, 'Hah, that will teach you to jump around like a lunatic and teach you to be flash.' So I thought, 'What do I do?' And I had no recourse but to completely look as though I meant to do it, so I smashed this guitar, broke it up. Jumped all over the bits and then picked up the 12-string and carried on as though nothing had happened. And the next day the place was packed; the next time we were there. And it just turned into another form of expression for me."

"I really am still a very crude player, and on a recording session one of the nice things is, I can drink half a bottle of brandy and spend a couple of hours experimenting. And often the best things that I do are accidents, complete accidents. Just go for it and see what happens. If I play a safe guitar solo, if I try and set out to do something safe, I can't pull it off. Because I haven't actually got any formal approach to it."

Pete Townshend 1978

66

"I can usually manage to get what I want to hear. I like being behind a desk in the studio and I like to be out on the floor in the studio and I like to come up with strings. I like to do bits and pieces of everything. I just have to slowly develop it. I'll never stop learning; it will take me a lifetime, but that will be good."

"As a guitar player I was always into other things. I never used to play a guitar much when I was with David; I would never bring a guitar around and play it. I would only play it when I was in the studio or on stage. I wanted to get into other things, and when I was in the studio I would always say, 'I don't want to play guitar yet.' Because it started becoming secondary to other things I wanted to do in the studio. Production, engineering . . . I really should have played it more than I did. I used to have to force myself to take it out sometimes, which was real strange for a guitar player."

Mick Ronson 1976

MICK RONSON | 1980

STEVE CLARK AND PHIL COLLEN | 1983

70

VIVIAN CAMPBELL | 1984

"I remember my hands bleeding on *Hysteria*. There would be blood on my right hand; it was a common thing."

Phil Collen 1995

"As a child, the guttural sound of the electric guitar captivated me. As a teen it consumed me, to such an extent that I devoted myself to exploring the art of trying to capture this lightning in a bottle. But it can never really be captured, only borrowed, and thus the tone of my playing was set. I fly by the seat of my pants; sometimes it's beautiful, sometimes it's painful, but it's seldom ever the same."

Vivian Campbell 2009

"There's a very important thing about being a rock and roll star and being a guitar player; I think there are only a few who have done both. But I think having the persona of being a rock and roll star is important. When you think of rock star you think of Jimmy Page holding up his double-neck."

"I definitely wanted to be a flashy guitar player, but I realized in the realms of Poison—I'm a songwriter, too—being a lead guitar player and a songwriter, they normally conflict. Because to write a great song and to have a great solo, very few times happens. And especially if you're the guitar player. If you're a guitar hero, you tend to write a song around the solo. Now, if you want to have a good song, you have to write a song. Instead of just coming up with these great chord changes and just putting lyrics somewhere near the beginning and the end."

C. C. Deville 1988

"I get hung up on some strange stuff—sometimes I'm happy, sometimes not. When I'm happy, that means being at one with the guitar. I guess that's a way of summing it up—to be one with it. Where it's genuinely an extension of you. I suppose that happens the more you work at it, the more you play."

"There is some pressure being a guitar hero. It can be terrifying, but I wasn't applying myself for the competition. It's not that I never wanted to be admired, but I didn't want it to get to the point where it wasn't a creative thing. I think it stops being a creative thing with some people."

Warren DeMartini 1986

JOEY ALLEN AND ERIK TURNER | 1991 ~ TOMMY SKEOCH AND FRANK HANNON | 1989

C. C. DEVILLE | 1986

74

C. C. DEVILLE | 1986 ~ WARREN DeMARTINI AND ROBBIN CROSBY | 1986

PAUL GILBERT | 2008 | 2001

"George Lynch is very, very intuitive, and you really get great magical moments because of that. I tend to be kind of math-y sometimes, which is nice in certain ways because I tend to know what I'm doing most of the time. I get really excited if I can do what George does, which is lose myself in the music and play something that is really inspired. He's a legend because of the style he created. When I heard him playing a lot of his licks, I thought, 'Man, he invented that style.' I learned it later; I'm a generation after George, but I remember copying those licks. He's one of the founding fathers of shred and metal."

Paul Gilbert 2009

"I wish I had more of the speed and accuracy. I know personally what I'm lacking, and I think that's what you need to progress. Whereas the feeling thing will always be there; it's not something you really have to exercise as much. It becomes harder and harder, especially if you don't have the basic tools, and I didn't grow up with the basic tools. I'm an ear player. I don't know a fucking note; I can't read a fucking note. I struggle over guitar notation. Try to learn the chords to 'Jump,' you know?"

"I change every few years. I listen to everyone and try to learn from everyone, but not sound like anyone."

George Lynch 1985

"I think George Lynch has got a brilliant style, a real authentic style. He's really been playing a long time, and what I genuinely admire about him is that he was playing while the things I was into were just happening. Without even seeing George play, I could hear the same things I was thinking about, which was to take the style of the earlier days and play it so that someone who liked it then could listen to you now."

Warren DeMartini 1986

"George Lynch is a great example of how to blend slow and fast shit together. He's fuckin' awesome; he has tons of feel. I think with a lot of the great rock guitar players, they're blues-based players anyway. There's a phrase and then there's all these blues notes in there, and then they'll pick their spots when they're gonna tear the guitar a new asshole. I think that's the whole key to it, you know?"

Zakk Wylde 2004

GEORGE LYNCH | 1983

80

BILLY DUFFY | 1989

82

ACE FREHLEY | 1976

"I always played lead in every group I was ever in. I picked up lead fast for some reason."

Ace Frehley 1978

"When we did our first album, there were a lot of things that I wasn't playing—notes or any kind of runs. Playing every night on and off for almost five years, you've got to get better. Your writing gets better as you can play better. You'll teach yourself something new on the guitar and incorporate it into songs. The better guitar player you are, the better your songs."

————————————

"Most lead players have a big deficiency when it comes to playing rhythm. Numerous times I'll talk to somebody and they'll say, 'Yeah, he's really a great lead player. But when you ask him to take over on rhythm, he falls apart.' I'd rather be an all-around guitar player; I'd rather be capable of doing either. I play more lead than I ever played, and it's something you grow at and something I don't think you really have to make an effort at."

Paul Stanley 1979

PAUL STANLEY | 1976

84

BRUCE KULICK | 1992

TOMMY THAYER | 2008

ANGUS YOUNG | 1982

88

ANGUS YOUNG | 1979

"I don't know too much about the technical side of guitar; I never bothered with it. If you know too much, it all becomes complex and then you start dissecting and analyzing. I just like thinking of it as good clean fun, you know? The only times I pick up a guitar is when I feel like playing, rather than six hours a day practice."

Angus Young 1978

"Getting the sound has always been the easiest part of the guitar. If you're playing it right, it's going to sound right somehow. I mean, you gladly turn down if it's going to sound good. It's not like, 'I have to have a wall of amps and a candelabra on top.' If you hit a chord and it's distorted, you clean it up. It's all what you hear."

"Malcolm will get something and I'll play along; it's a natural thing. I suppose it's just something we do well together. He seems to have a great command of rhythm, and he likes doing that. That to me is more important because if we're playing live and something goes wrong with my gear and my guitar drops out, you can still hear him and it's not empty. He's probably got the best right hand in the world. I've never heard anyone do it like that; even Keith Richards or any of those people. As soon as the other guitar drops out, it's empty. But with Malcolm it's so full. Besides, Malcolm always said that playing lead interfered with his drinkin', and so he said I should do it."

Angus Young 1983

MALCOLM YOUNG | 1976

ANGUS YOUNG | 1983

STEVE MORSE | 1998

"I'm really into different sounds because I get bored easily. Going from one solo to another in tunes, I try to act like there was two different guitarists."

Steve Morse 1984

"My philosophy with guitar solos is that I think they should be musical; I don't think they should be a lull in the song. They should keep the song up and they should be a musical interlude that's interesting. And it should go along with the mood of the song. It should carry the mood the way a vocalist would, just as interesting and appropriate for the song."

John Petrucci 1997

"I personally prefer a lot of taste instead of going mad on the guitar; I like to use a lot of taste and putting the right notes together to make them very melodic."

"If you learn from a teacher, he influences you. If you do it on your own, you start learning to play the guitar and you start bringing your own style to it straight from the beginning."

"There's so much I do automatically; I do it without thinking. So I have to think about what I'm doing and compare myself to other guitarists and what they do to see if something I do is special."

Michael Schenker 1977

96

MICHAEL SCHENKER | 1978

RUDOLPH SCHENKER AND MATTHIAS JABS | 1986

ADRIAN SMITH | 1987

DAVE MURRAY | 1987

K. K. DOWNING AND GLENN TIPTON | 1984

"What happens is, being two different guitar players anyway, and you have a chord sequence—C—Dm—F—we'll play 'em in different positions. And I think that's a big part of the band's sound. If something's lacking you go, 'Well, why don't you play a different inversion?' and you just get a fuller sound. More texture."

"If there's a two-part solo, swapping solo, and if I do the first one, I'll think to myself, 'Right, I'm really gonna set the standard here. Glenn's really gonna have to come up with it!' And it works good on the other end because if Glenn puts something down then I'll think to myself, 'Right, I'm gonna burn the shit out of that!' And that's the way it works; it's a pretty healthy competition."

"I've never been able to get a good sound out of a Marshall amp or a Gibson Flying V by plugging straight into the amplifier. Not the sound that I look for. So it's basically the effects in-between the guitar and the amplifier that do most of the work for my particular sound."

K. K. Downing 1984

"Each album for me seems to set me off in a different direction lead-wise. I always considered that I have got my own style and I'm easily identifiable as a guitarist, but I still need to find new areas to explore. It gives my style, not a different direction, but an added flavor."

"I've never placed a great deal of importance on speed, although I can play relatively fast. I do place a lot of importance on feel and interest and taste in the guitar. Not just for myself, but that's the sign of a good guitarist: a guitarist that plays well within his means. He's not trying to play a blur of notes that he's not quite capable of playing. . . . I think a good guitarist is somebody who plays quite well below his limits."

Glenn Tipton 1986

102

ROBIN TROWER | 1975

"I think there used to be a lot more kind of guitar heroes, your Eddie Van Halens and guys like that. When I was growing up, there were a lot of really talented lead players, your more pyrotechnic kinds of players that could just rip your face off. Technically really proficient guys. I think it's gone a lot more toward songwriting; I don't think I've seen that in a while. In our music, I don't really wank off a whole lot either as far as soloing. And that's the kind of school I come from. But I also took a few classes in Yngwie Malmsteen and Eddie Van Halen, and I enjoyed that stuff."

"I wanted to be up there doing my solo and all that kind of stuff. But then I got into Alice, and I always came from the dual guitar bands. I really like the dual guitar bands, the British metal bands like Iron Maiden, Scorpions, Judas Priest, Thin Lizzy, and even Lynyrd Skynyrd. I like dual guitars; I started off playing rhythm and I like rhythm. I started from there and then I got into a phase where I got into your technically more proficient cats. I kind of went that route for a while, but this was all in my search to find myself."

Jerry Cantrell 1998

"I'm really influenced by Hendrix, I'm the first to admit it. Anybody who has got any ears and plays the guitar couldn't not be influenced by Hendrix. It's like you can't write unless you learn a-b-c. His was the most universal statement on guitar ever, when everybody else was just fucking about. He made real music on the guitar; it just wasn't licks on top of somebody else's music. He played total music. That's where I think my biggest influence from Hendrix comes from—the attitude towards making music is what I got from him."

Robin Trower 1974

"I think technique has always been a dangerous thing in rock and roll."

"I must have had a desire to be a guitar hero. You must have ambition to achieve anything. You want what you do to be liked. If they didn't dig it, I'd be at home sweeping the roads. I'm only able to carry on because people like it."

Robin Trower 1986

104

SCOTT GORHAM | 1979

JOHN SYKES | 1984

106

"I was a huge Clapton fan. The fire and the aggression of his playing; the sheer beauty of the sound."

"I was just awed by Clapton's tone. I was really young, but the first time I heard it was when Cream first came out, but then I went back and heard Bluesbreakers. I just freaked out. Some of it was the equipment, but really more than that, I think it was his intent when he was playing. And he was pushing that out of his guitar, and it didn't really matter what he used. That was his sound. The sound was so amazing. God! And then Fresh Cream and his tone was like . . . that was enough sound to last a lifetime for me. And it's not that there couldn't be other sounds, and people would go on and do this and that. It's like other people would hear Charlie Parker and go, 'That's it, that's enough tone for my lifetime.' And that's kind of the way it was with Clapton's tone. It was kind of like that natural EQ tone that you'd find on an old violin."

Eric Johnson 2004

"I've always admired Eric's playing, going all the way back to when I was a little kid; Cream and all that stuff. I was always aware of Eric's place in the pantheon of great musicians."

"'Me and Mr. Johnson' is probably my favorite aspect of Clapton's playing; the authenticity that he brings to straight-up blues playing. And he's only gotten better over the years, too. He was always great, but his recent work is his best."

"I think everybody would agree Eric [Clapton] is about the music; I mean he doesn't do anything fancy, he's not doing somersaults or anything like that. He basically plays the guitar and sings his ass off, and it's a testament to one thing, and that's the quality of the work that he's done. I think it's very simply about that and only that, and that's enough to kind of give you hope right there. He's very rightly earned a very unique, a very special place in the spectrum of artists. And it's only about one thing—that he delivers great music."

Pat Metheny 2004

ERIC CLAPTON | 1975

PAT METHENY | 1981

112

AL DI MEOLA | 1980 ~ PACO DE LUCÍA | 1996

"I think Edward Van Halen is great; he has a beautiful spirit, too. He does nice things on the guitar. Stanley Jordan I'm very fond of; Allan Holdsworth as well. When I hear a guitarist, I want to hear what he's doing with my instrument. There's nothing I love more than to hear somebody play my instrument in a way I'd never dreamed of before. I'm very demanding as a listener and a player, and when I listen I say, 'What is this player doing?'"

––––––––––––––––––––––

"If someone thinks I play fast, they should hear John Coltrane. I mean, he just rips up and down that horn, and the notes fall out like a cascade. It's all just a feeling, and I'd like to be able to articulate that feeling on the guitar. You can do anything with work. Anything is possible, and it's up to you. If you're willing to spend hours working, devoting and dedicating yourself to the articulation and execution, then sooner or later you're going to come through."

John McLaughlin circa mid-1980s

"I can't bang or throw my guitar on the floor because I love guitars. And I won't set it on fire. That's me. I'm one of those guys who plays with a natural guitar sound: Nothing on it, no fuzz, no wah-wah, nothing. Pure guitar playing using contemporary music, a little R&B. That's me. It sounded unique in a world where there was none."

––––––––––––––––––––––

"I think we've got more great guitar players today than we've ever had. They may not be as great because today we don't have the demand on their greatness or their abilities like we did years ago. Django Reinhardt. Les Paul was and still is a great guitar player. Tal Farlowe, one of my very favorites. I like Carlos Santana's playing. Jeff Beck. Larry Carlton is one of the finest players in the world today. John McLaughlin. Al Di Meola."

George Benson 1980

"I work with a lot of blues, and where blues has led other forms of music. If you know how to play the blues, how to change with the chords, transitions, then you're getting into jazz. If you can do blues and jazz with feeling, you can do rock. If you can only do jazz, there's no way you can do rock. Take George Benson; he's the greatest technician for jazz today, and he's got a lot of feeling. He's one of my favorite, primo, all-time guitar players, and if he tries to play rock scales or bend notes, it's just dumb. I try to be as versatile a guitarist as I can. I'll fuckin' play it if it's a good tune. You can't be afraid of change."

Frank Marino 1978

115

116

"My background is a blues background. I inherited my first guitar from my grandfather, who was a spiritualist preacher and a minister and he played guitar, and when he died I inherited his guitar. My grandma gave me his guitar and told me, 'Don't play any blues on the guitar'; that was a provision. I told her, 'Oh, grandmother, I definitely will not,' and it wasn't two days before I was playing some blues, man! I couldn't wait to get it home to start trying to learn to play me some blues. Which I did, man. I listened to artists like T-Bone Walker and Lowell Fulson and Gatemouth Brown; Gatemouth was really my inspiration, I think, and my whole concept is based around him. I play with a clamp [capo] and no pick, and it's really his style of playing. That's really the foundation of what I first started to do."

Johnny "Guitar" Watson 1979

"Within the blues, you can play near jazz or very low down and play it funky. But it's like picking a different menu every day though—the blues is a wide range of music one can do and still be within the blues. So you get many directions to go with the blues."

"I like many instruments; guitar is not the only instrument I like. It's the only one I can play pretty well, but I've tried to play clarinet, violin, piano, bass; keep a little time on the drums, a little harmonica. I can't hear very well; any very low notes don't cut through to me; I miss 'em. So I play high (on the neck) all the time; that I can hear. Like the bass or the piano, if they play too low, I won't know where it is. The treble on a guitar I can hear better, but I hear a lot of guys playing—Charlie Christian, Django Reinhardt, and many other guys—that is really playin' good jazz; they play with a little bit more bass. It sounds good to me, but I can't make mine sound like that and sound good to me."

"I was in Twist, Arkansas, and while I was playing there one night the place caught on fire, and I ran back in trying to save my guitar. And I almost lost my life trying to save it. We found the two guys who started the fire, and they were fighting about a lady named Lucille. I never did meet her, but I named my guitar Lucille, and that reminded me not to do anything like that again."

B.B. King circa mid-1970s

"Now, I think my biggest influence, as a guitar player, is definitely B.B. King. Until I heard B.B. King, I was going along one way, and then I completely switched directions."

Robin Trower 1974

118

JOHNNY "GUITAR" WATSON | 1981

120

CHUCK BERRY | 1973

122

FREDDIE KING | 1976

123

"I like the Chicago blues from the '50s the best. I try to sound like that all the time. Howlin' Wolf, Muddy Waters—those were the main two. What I do is just electrified Mississippi delta stuff, just rougher and rawer."

—————————

"You can pretty much go wherever you want to with the blues. It's still as much fun for me now as it's always been. It means a lot to me; I love playing it."

Johnny Winter 2005

126

RORY GALLAGHER | 1982 | 1973

"I like to keep that acoustic approach. I mean, I like to have electronics, sure, but I'm just into the guitar. I don't want to get into the so-called popular blues style—playing single notes and then turning your guitar down and singing. I'm into getting as much out of the guitar as possible, which was the original idea of the guitar. I'm almost, if you will, into the classical approach to the guitar like Segovia had of getting everything you can out of the guitar by the use of all the fingers and all the means you can get. There's a million things in there to come out. Sometimes you can get them out with an electronic device, but that's the beauty of the instrument."

"I just use my hands, the guitar, and amp. I like to use harmonics. The Fender neck has these overtones up and down the entire length, and you can use this to sort of muffle notes. On the lower part of the neck, I muffle with the finger and the pick, and it causes the note to sound like a synthesizer. When you ping notes higher up the neck, it sounds like they're in a tape loop and are coming out backwards. I've been doing it for years. It depends on the tone and how much you really want to get them out. You can get a lot of interesting effects from it."

"I just try and get a volume whereby the guitar is still almost of an acoustic nature. You know, if you just hit that a little harder, you can get a hard note, and if you hit quite soft, you can get a soft sound. I still like to get that acoustic feel about the guitar. Does that sound crazy? I don't like to see a guy hit a note and then turn up his volume control and let that do the work. I just like to go wooomph and really dig the note. For an introduction or solo, I have my guitar up to 10 or maybe $9\frac{1}{2}$ to give myself a little room, and then from the rhythm guitar I'd have it at about $7\frac{1}{2}$ or 8. I control the sound—a clean solo sound, for instance—by lowering the volume on the guitar. Then, for chording, I turn the guitar volume back up full to achieve a fuzzy tone."

Rory Gallagher 1974

RORY GALLAGER | 1974 | 1977

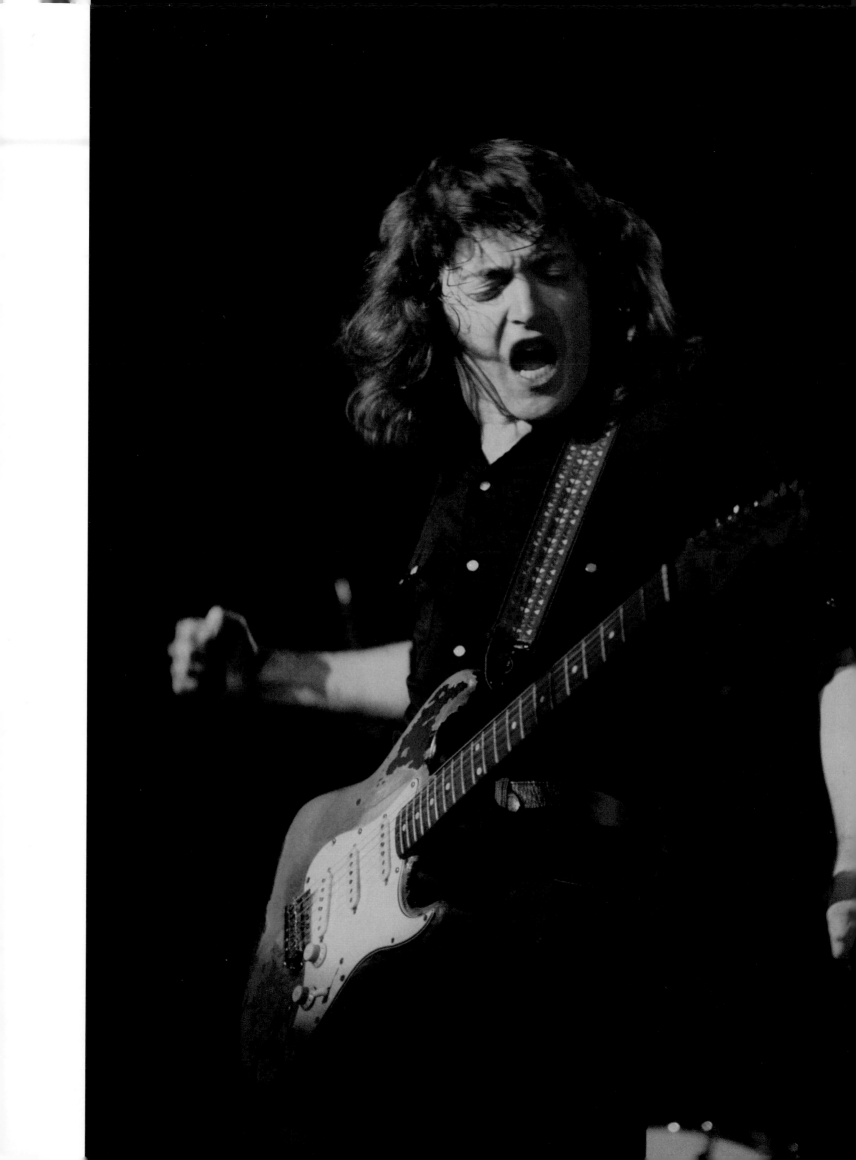

132

134

135

"I think if you're playing blues music, you have to sing because it's like a call and response thing. Regardless of how my voice sounds, whether it's good or bad, I found my own voice, but more than that, it's helped me redefine my own guitar style. When you're actually singing the blues yourself, in between the vocal phrases, you're answering your voice with your own guitar and it becomes a much more personal, expressive thing."

Mick Taylor 1990

"I was the lead guitarist; I had that label. That was at the time when people used to think there were special guitars for rhythm and special guitars for leads."

"Half the time, Eric thinks he's terrible. Except when he's good, he knows he's good, you know. Which is great, you know, he celebrates the fact that he was good. I like that. All guitarists do a bit, you know. If it comes off good, they know there's no denying that it came off good and that's it. And have a drink to that. And Jimmy Page is like that too—he's very critical of his playing, but if he plays something good, he knows it's there."

"I've been lifted up because I don't know where the guitar is going to take me, you know. The good thing about the guitar is you don't know where you're going next if you don't practice; which I never get the chance to. The only chance is when you're working on something over and over again in the studio or live gigs. But it seems to have a way of creeping up on you when you're sleeping or something. You get a new vantage point, you know, when you wake up."

Ron Wood 1975

"There are a lot of good lead players but not a whole lot of good rhythm players. Oddly enough, I've never really emulated the Stones, but I think that Keith Richards is a compelling rhythm player. And John Lennon is a lot like that, too. I think John Lennon is an amazing rhythm guitarist. He knows how to be loosely tight, if I can put it that way. Jimmy Page is like that. But John Lennon, especially—he's just got more soul than he can handle almost. David Gilmour is another incredible player who does both great: rhythms and leads."

Nancy Wilson 1979

JOHN MAYALL | 1969

138

ERIC SARDINAS | 2000

"I think ultimately it's the connection between the instrument and the player. Traditional blues, whether it's pre-war blues like Blind Lemon Jefferson, Robert Johnson, Son House, and Charlie Patton, or it's Chicago blues like Elmore James and Tampa Red—the spirit of blues is so close to the human heartbeat. And I think that organic connection that happens between instrument and player is really a powerful energy."

"The slide is very emotional; it really resonates the human voice. I think it's really about what's in between the lines a lot of times. The way I look at music and the peaks and valleys that happen organically when the music is going, I think the slide really connects those spots for me."

"I have traditional instruments that I've pushed out of their traditional element. I just naturally created my own sound of who I am from the essence of those inspirations coming through and making those fibers come together. Electrify. I started playing acoustic guitar when I was like six; I always liked acoustic guitar. And when I started gravitating towards electric guitar—though I loved Les Pauls and Strats and all of that—it was hollowbodies, because they resonated a lot of that acoustic energy."

"Traditional blues, the essence of slide guitar, and the connection between the slide resonating and the human voice sounds so sweet to me. It sounds so sweet to me on Resonator guitars, and when I got hold of that, that was really the sound I liked. When I was a kid, I just started getting pickups drilled into them, not really knowing what I was doing. So, to me it's my acoustic guitar and it's also my electric."

Eric Sardinas 2009

BILLIE JOE ARMSTRONG | 2004

KENNY WAYNE SHEPHERD | 1997

142

SLASH | **1987** | **1988** | **2007** | **1989**

"Whenever I hang out with guitar players, the last thing we want to talk about is guitars. I think guitar players are an interesting breed because we're all very aware of how many of us there are and we're also very aware of what the other guys are doing or what their sound is like and blah blah blah. But it's almost like a magician kind of thing: no one really talks about what they do. I'd actually think it was rude if I was to inquire too much as to what Jimmy has got in his guitar or Billy Gibbons has got in his guitar or Joe has got in his guitar."

"For me personally, I don't know what it is that I do. I don't know if I could stand back from it. I know there are certain things I do that are very identifiable to me . . . but I don't know too many different combinations of things that I do that I could really stand back and go, 'Well, you have to do this and this and this.' I'm way too insecure a guitar player to even go there!"

"I love what I do. I've always been excited about it . . . Just the fact that you can get up and play. You have a guitar or more than one guitar, and that you've got access to be able to play all the time is a blessing."

"When I first started, I was busy with the task at hand, which was just learning how to play. Which still seems to be the case. I didn't have any sort of far-reaching goals. I guess because I've persevered over the years, I've probably just stuck around for so long that I've finally been recognized as someone who won't go away."

"I've always been more into the old players. That might be kind of a drawback, but I always tried to grow and extend from there. I wanted to grow on my own and come up with my own things. So I got the basic structure from those kinds of players, but from there I just worked on my own; just teaching myself."

Slash 2007

146

IZZY STRADLIN | 1987

"When you really want to get down to the honest to God truth and you want to make someone laugh or cry, it's still the guitar. The guitar is a phenomenal instrument because you can make it talk. With a saxophone, you have something in your mouth so you can't talk, and you can only play one note at a time; the piano player has his back turned to the audience; and the drummer is anything but musical. And it goes on and on and on. The guitar is something you can take on the beach, put on the plane, take it to the bedroom . . . and if you have a fight with your wife, it's the first thing you reach for. It's a psychiatrist, a maid, a prostitute; it's everything."

Les Paul 1978

"Leo Fender would come over to the place on Curson Street, and so would his engineers. And they saw the Log; they saw the guitars that I had built; they saw me pounding them out on the pavement; they saw me working the Headless Wonder. They saw all this happening."

"Between 1941, when I designed the guitar that came out as the Les Paul guitar, and 1951, Gibson kind of tacked the name on me, [the guy with the] 'broomstick with the pickups on it.' And from 1941 until 1951, I couldn't convince Gibson to do a damn thing about putting out a Les Paul guitar. It took Leo Fender to pick up on that idea from my garage in the backyard. Leo decided to come out with the Fender line, and immediately Gibson says, 'Find the character with the broomstick with the pickups on it.' So they asked me to design a guitar. I thank Leo for coming out with his because it woke Gibson up. Gibson was asleep; Fender was not asleep. And of course that's the way it goes."

Les Paul 1984

"Les Paul was around before all these fucking guys. That motherfucker had some fuckin' chops back then, and there was no distortion then, man. I've seen some old footage of him playing with Mary Ford, and it was like, 'Holy shit.' It was like Yngwie before Yngwie; a 1950s version of Yngwie."

Zakk Wylde 2004

LES PAUL | 1981

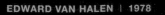
EDWARD VAN HALEN | 1978

"I really don't know how to explain this, man. I was just sittin' in my room at the pad, at home, drinking a beer, and I remember seeing people just stretching one note and hitting the note once. And I said, 'Well, fuck, man, nobody's really capitalizing on that. I mean nobody is really doing more than just one stretch and one note real quick.' So I just started dickin' around and said, 'Fuck, this is a totally other technique that nobody really does.' A lot of people listen to 'Eruption' and they don't even think it's a guitar. 'What is that, man? Synthesizer? Piano?'"

Edward Van Halen 1979

"The brown sound is basically a tone, a feeling that I'm always working at. Everything is involved in that, and I've been working with it since I've been playing. It comes from the person."

Edward Van Halen 1985

"Hearing Eddie doing 'Spanish Fly,' it was like, 'Jesus Christ, how can anybody play like that?' Then it was Randy because he was after Ed, and I thought it was damn cool shit; Ozzy's new guitar player was fuckin' awesome. And then my buddy said, 'Dude, are you sitting down? You've got to hear this.' I remember the first time I heard Yngwie play and I was like, 'You've got to be fuckin' joking.' It was like a pissed off Al Di Meola playing rock guitar with chops like that. Yngwie opened up a whole thing for that. Because they always just considered rock guitar players sloppy, fucking crappy players. Whereas jazz/fusion guys were the guys who had chops. From Eddie onward it turned into, 'If you want to play rock guitar, you've gotta fuckin' know how to play your instrument.'"

Zakk Wylde 2004

"One of the things about Van Halen was not just Eddie; I love his guitar playing, and he was someone I don't even try to touch. I've learned 'Unchained' and 'Panama,' and they're really fun, but it's not easy to learn those songs. But once you learned them, you feel like you really accomplished something. But also, Van Halen was a tight unit. Being in the Donnas and the Chelsea Girls, I don't ever want to be fazed by something where there are two guitars. Van Halen were the ultimate four-piece where the singer doesn't play any instrument and they sound full and tight; the drumming is just as catchy as the bass playing, which is just as catchy as the guitar playing. I like a lot of bands with two guitar players just as well, but there's just something kind of cool when there's just one guitar player covering it all."

Allison Robertson 2009

154

156

EDWARD VAN HALEN | 1978 | 1981

"Dimebag is, if not *the* favorite, *is* one of my favorite guitar players. His uncanny feel; he has more feel than anybody that's ever picked up a guitar. It's just what he does. He just rapes and pillages the guitar, he tortures it. You listen to some of those songs and it's like, 'How can you do that on an instrument?' You know, when I was maybe 19 or 20 or 21, if somebody told me I couldn't be like Dimebag Darrell I probably would've said, 'Fuck you, yes I can.' But now I am what I am and hopefully kids dig on that."

Synyster Gates 2007

159

DIMEBAG DARRELL | 1995 | 1997

160

"I found the guitar very hard at first; it was very difficult. The first six months were difficult, and then it became very easy; then after about three years it became very difficult again."

"I don't like recording too much; it's too clinical. A lot of people love it; they can edit their music and put it together and make it nice, but when they get onstage they're lost. My way of thinking is the opposite. I love to have that freedom of just going onstage and playing whatever I want to play at the time. I'll play the numbers I'm supposed to play, but in the in-between parts if I'm feeling good, I'll play something completely off the wall that I've never ever played in my life."

"I think I got to a stage where I was thinking, 'I still haven't proved myself yet. I still want to be more and more and more.' I never got very much emotion out of Deep Purple music. I did when I was onstage. Except for *Machine Head* and *In Rock*, there wasn't a lot that moved me about what we did, and I could never figure out why. It was just misinterpretation between the guitar and the vocalist most of the time, which wasn't their fault. I just had a very bad way of explaining myself of what I wanted put over the top. Plus, it got to the stage where I couldn't really tell a singer what to sing. I didn't want to. He's the singer—he should sing whatever he feels."

Ritchie Blackmore 1975

"I don't practice specific things; I practice avenues of playing to try and lose myself in the guitar. I don't think you should be thinking too heavily about what you're playing. And lots of times when I'm playing the guitar, I don't really know what I'm doing or where I am. I'm just going up and down the guitar rather than looking at each note and thinking 'That's an E.' And other times I stop completely and just go *ohhhh* in frustration. It's whether I'm inspired; being an extremist, I go from being totally uninspired to very inspired."

Ritchie Blackmore 1978

"Solos are the easiest thing. Songs, I mean to write songs, that's the hard thing. Whenever I write a song, I think of the riff and the chord progression, and hence the arrangement kind of works. The last thing I think of is the solo, and sometimes we've finished songs and I have to go in and do the solo and I've kind of forgotten what everything is about. It's strange sometimes. I know that other guitar players write from the point of view of what they've learned, what they're good at. If something is very flashy they'll build a song around something flashy. I just don't think like that."

Ritchie Blackmore 1997

163

164

RITCHIE BLACKMORE | 1974

TOMMY BOLIN | 1976

166

NANCY WILSON | 1983

"My favorite era was actually the Cream, *Wheels of Fire* era, because that album was very influential on myself as far as learning how to improvise and to stretch out a bit . . . It was a tone, a voice, and soul, you know?"

Neal Schon 2004

"My hands are the true story of my personality. One hand looks kind of glamorous, and the other is a real worker hand with the broken nails."

"Paul Simon was a big influence as an acoustic, fingerstyle player. When I first started on electric, Jimmy Messina was a big influence. Also Jeff Beck and Jimmy Page. I have been exposed to so many kinds of music since I was very young—there have been classical, rock, and all sorts of things. Not a whole lot of jazz, but there's some jazz that's really great. Steve Howe is another big influence."

"When we were first getting going, other guitar players used to come up to me and say, 'You don't play too bad—for a girl.' Well, too bad I'm a girl, I guess. I mean, what can I say to that? People say, 'It sure looks funny to see a girl up there with this big red Stratocaster wailing away.' It's much more 'acceptable' to see a woman playing acoustic guitar, but even that has brought some comments. Like the intro to 'Crazy on You' has some aggressive playing on it."

Nancy Wilson 1979

"Soloing is about inspiration. It's about wanting to obtain something, wanting to reach something. It's knowing how to go about reaching it that's called experience. Obviously that's what people who don't know how to do what I do don't have. Because if they had experience, they might know how to do it."

"I constantly fought to be a guitarist, who after 1967, never played a blues phrase in my life. I've gone back on that a few times, but hardly even in the '70s did I do, *Duh-duh-duh-deeeee* [sings blues lick]. And 90 percent of all guitarists did exactly that, so I was fighting back, and that was the best thing I ever did for my career. I love blues, and particularly Big Bill Broonzy and many other great blues guitarists, particularly country blues guitarists. To me, the blues was really important, but I didn't want to play it."

Steve Howe 2006

ELVIS COSTELLO | 1977

172

KURT COBAIN | 1992

"I think being a good musician is something that's gotten lost nowadays because you had the punk rock aesthetic and people thought it wasn't cool to practice their instruments and be a good musician. And that's just bullshit. The instrument is a thing to make colorful sounds on, and you can work on it to get better and better. Practice doesn't mean you play faster; it's just learning how to play better with people."

John Frusciante 1999

"Sometimes live in the Chili Peppers I get into that flashy rockstar lead guitar thing, but it's more because of the energy of playing in front of an audience. It's not something that I'm interested in musically; it's more something I do because I get off on the interaction between the audience and the excitement that's generated in the exchange of love."

"I can recognize most of my favorite guitar players playing. There's something that makes people's muscles and skin and the electricity in an individual's body like no one else. You can hear somebody like Jeff Beck playing one note and you know who it is. As I've grown as a musician, I've gotten more comfortable with sounding like myself."

John Frusciante 2004

174

176

JOAN JETT | 1976

LITA FORD | 1991

"I wanted to start a band—it had nothing to do with sex or fame or excitement. When a song hit different chord changes, I could feel it in my soul."

"At first, I didn't really worry about solos as much. Then when I started soloing more and doing a lot of lead work, people started calling me a lead guitar player all the time. It's not that I don't want to be considered that as well, but when I was younger I'd always remind people, 'I'm really more of a rhythm player.' I'm really holdin' down rhythm with the rest of the girls, and then I take a solo here and there. I love rhythm playing; to me, sometimes it can be more difficult than playing solos."

"Being a female in a band works both ways: it's something working for you and something working against you. A lot of females have chips on their shoulders, but I've always felt like it was an advantage because it's a gimmick, whether you want to admit it or not. Even if you don't mean it to be a gimmick, it just is. You do stand out by being female, which is good because you're a little bit separate from the pack, but at the same time, you get a lot of scrutiny and comparisons to other females. And that's always frustrating because there are a lot of different kinds of guitar players, but when you're a female guitarist, you immediately get compared to the only other female players that exist."

"I actually feel kind of honored that I don't get compared to other female guitarists; I think that's like a compliment. I hope people just think of me as having my own style, which has nothing to do with me being a girl or how other girl bands might influence me. If someone heard our record, I've always wanted someone to think, 'Who's that guy playing guitar?' You don't want people picturing a girl playing, and who knows what that looks like in your head? In the Donnas, we've always said we wanted to sound like a bunch of mountain men with big beards playing on the album. And not just a bunch of girls."

Allison Robertson 2009

180

BONNIE RAITT | 1978

CHRISSIE HYNDE | 1980

"Jimi and I started hanging out together when he came over from Monterey, and we went down to my place at the beach in Malibu. And like played for two days, something ridiculous like that; playing to the ocean. We must have made up like four albums' worth of actual songs; I mean they were songs, all you needed to do was work on the lyrics and stuff. The cops came and asked to see my lease, and they said, 'Listen, if you walk out and there's four cop cars, don't be alarmed. All we're gonna do is listen 'cause it's just as groovy to sit here and listen for our calls as to sit up on top of the hill.' Sure enough, there were three highway patrolmen and two sheriff cars just diggin' it, man. I said, 'Wow! Far out!'"

Stephen Stills 1978

"To me, the whole thread of meaning through American popular music was to get louder. When they found out a broken speaker sounded louder, that was a great stride. And it was taken to a level where you could no longer achieve that volume; you couldn't record it. And then you discovered the little amp with the mike turned all the way up sounds louder than the big amp turned all the way down. How you get that heavy metal thing to sound big is not so easy."

"I don't do things in a kind of normal, orderly fashion."

"I watched Steve Vai on the *Crossroads* film and how he did it, and that was interesting; he had sussed it out. Because loud is not always loud; loud is sometimes little."

Ry Cooder 1995

RY COODER | 1981

184

"John Lee Hooker told me, 'If you want to be a good guitar player, take all the notes and play half as many as you would. And you'll be on your way to doing something.'"

"I was always hearing this music in my head, and far-out music. It's a wonderful, wonderful thing. It's like the sun and the rain; it's a paradise. And the thing is to get it out of my head. I'm not a good enough instrumentalist to truly express what I hear and feel in my mind. But I practiced a lot, and the more I practiced the closer I got to really communicating what was in my head."

"I loved the blues, and there were some great electric blues players. But I just didn't feel like there was a home for me on the electric Strat. And if I was gonna play an electric, I'd wanna play a Strat. The electric didn't cry for me. That's the beauty of the slide; the slide cries. And you come into the world crying, know what I mean? For me on the electric, I was just whinin'. And that's what most contemporary electric guitarists are doing today—they're just whining. And they're copying Muddy Waters or Robert Johnson or Elmore James."

"When I think about electric instruments, I think about perfection —I think about Hendrix."

Ben Harper 1995

"I listened to Hendrix, Page, Dave Gilmour; blues guys, B.B. King, Albert King, everybody. And even guys you wouldn't even think of like session players; the Motown players and Stax players. Just records in general. I listened to so many different kinds of records. I just picked out stuff and learned about that style through that."

Lenny Kravitz 1995

186

PRINCE | 1985

188

CHET ATKINS | 1995

"I knew I wanted to be a guitar player when I was about five years old. A friend of the family was outside and doing some work around the house. He picked up a guitar and started playing some old blues stuff. I said, 'What sound is that?' He had this little amp plugged in and this old distorted guitar and he was playing some Howlin' Wolf stuff."

Eric Johnson 1996

"People come up to me and say I have this original style, and it's really not so much true. It's really just derivative of all the people I like. If you're just twice or three times removed from the original point, all of a sudden it's hard to tell that it's like the original."

Eric Johnson 2004

"I've never been very comfortable in the studio; it's really hard work because I never play anything the same way twice. I'm an improviser."

Chet Atkins 1990

"In Creedence, I became much more of a writer. I thought I was a pretty good guitar player then, but I was sort of a pedestrian guitar player; I wasn't a great guitar player. I was good enough for the job. I never like worried about it too much, and that was part of the problem; I became so successful and I was steered over to the songwriting, 'cause we all know you need the material. At least, that's what I always thought, you need songs. You're wasting space if you're just waiting for the solo to get here."

John Fogerty 1997

JOHN FOGERTY | **2005**

192

WAYLON JENNINGS | 1977

193

"I play from emotion. I've never consciously tried to be a flash. Emotion rules everything I do."

"Feedback was unavoidable. Playing in small clubs, you always got feedback because of bad systems, and really the electrical thing hadn't been sewn up. All the amps were underpowered and screwed up full volume and always whistling. My amp was always whistling. I'd kick it and bash it and a couple of tubes would break, and I was playing largely on an amp with just one output valve still working. It would feed back, so I decided to use it rather than fight it. It was hopeless to try and play a chord because it would just *rrrrr.* So then when I progressed onto a bigger amp and I didn't get it, I kind of missed it. I went to hit a note and there wasn't any distortion; too clean. It was horrible. So the ideal thing was to get the beauty of the feedback but controllable feedback."

"I can understand Mahavishnu because they've done what I wanted to do, really. McLaughlin is far more technically knowledgeable. I mean, I don't know half of what he knows. I don't know chords; I mean I just never had to worry about those kinds of chords because they weren't usable. McLaughlin wouldn't come and watch me, let me tell you."

Jeff Beck 1973

"Jeff is excellent; he's one of my very favorites. Among all the guitar players that I know of in the rock field, Jeff Beck has more taste and more going for him than any of them. I think the guy plays great; I really do. From the time I first heard Jeff, I liked his playing very much. One of the things that attracted me to him was his consistency, and the second thing was his phrasing. And the heart that he played with. And this is very important because when I first heard some of the rock players, they were just playing notes and not saying much. And this is where Jeff doesn't have to necessarily play a fast run to prove a point."

Les Paul 1978

"I was really influenced by Beck. He was like the first person to play in that Indian style. He made his guitar sound like different instruments, and no one else was doing that."

Gary Moore 1984

"If you hold your guitar against the amp, you might get a harmonic feedback, or you might get nothing. But that's what interests me: playing with electricity. Like I can turn on some jazz guitarist, and he won't do a thing for me if he's not playing electrically. But Jeff Beck's great to listen to because he takes a chance and when it comes off, it's so emotional. When he gets feedback going right, it's just like an orchestra playing instead of just a guitar with a lot of brilliant runs. Actually, the real art of chance music is knowing what to do if you don't get what you tried for. Like if a ballet dancer falls over, it's knowing how to get out of looking clumsy that counts. Beck takes a chance every night. Sometimes, he's absolutely useless, and you wonder why he's got a name. Other times he pulls things off that sound like nothing you've ever heard before. He's one of my favorite guitarists. But taking all those chances is why he gets such bad reviews sometimes. The reviewers sometimes catch him on nights when it doesn't work. The kind of things that you do in that kind of playing are subconscious and depend on what type of day you've had and things like that. If I've read a lot, or if I've had a game of chess and my mind's working, I can play much better than if I've had a lazy day of sitting in a car or plane. But also, I just think there are good days and bad days, all having nothing to do with the cycle of life."

Ritchie Blackmore 1978

196

"I got into a heavy blues period when I discovered what those three chords were that B.B. King was doing. That was a big revelation to me, so I played along with those records for hours and hours."

"There've been a few players—Eddie Van Halen, Robben Ford, Warren, and Pat Metheny—who I took all their solos and put 'em back to back on a tape just so I could listen to them. I couldn't even tell you what songs they were from because I just knew the solos."

"Ed brought me back to rock. I went through the folk period when I was younger and then a heavy blues period, then into pop-rock. When I went to G.I.T., I switched over to bebop—Joe Pass, Joe Diorio, and that kind of thing. When Van Halen came out, it took me a while to get into him because I was such a jazz Nazi, I guess. But when I finally got into him, it was mind-blowing."

Jennifer Batten 1987

"I listen to quite a few guitar players, but I don't want to cop any of their stuff because I don't want people saying, 'Where did you get that from?' I listen to Beck, Blackmore, Schenker, all those big boys."

198

Mick Mars 1983

JENNIFER BATTEN | 1992

MICK MARS | 1984

"One of the main things that I really wanted to try to do is really have my own unique style. To have my own kind of thing where people go, 'Oh, well that sounds like John 5.' Clapton and Jimmy Page, they have their own thing because they are truly originals. Steve Vai said, 'It takes balls to be a true original,' and I think that's what I was really reaching for. He said I'm an underrated guitar giant, a true original, and I think that's the best compliment anybody has ever given me because that's what I've been trying to do."

"I really like Van Halen's tone; it's undeniable. I really like the ZZ Top tone on like 'Cheap Sunglasses.' That's the epitome of a great tone. And then I think of Led Zeppelin and things like that. I really try and get that great tone where you can listen to it really loud and it still sounds good. Those are the real professionals: Jimmy Page and Billy Gibbons and Jeff Beck got that tone where it would actually rip your heart out. What comes out of that guy's fingers is unbelievable."

John 5 2004

JAMES HETFIELD AND KIRK HAMMETT | 1989

204

JEFF HANNEMAN AND KERRY KING | 1998

206

MICK THOMSON AND JIM ROOT | 2004

SYNYSTER GATES AND ZACKY VENGEANCE | 2007

"I couldn't tell you what distinguishes my playing. I just try not to fit in any particular place. But I do tend to look at the past. To me, the most influential players are the ones who you can tell who it is just by hearing their guitar tone or their phrasing. There are a lot of guys out there that can tear it up, but you can't tell one from the other. I like to go against what people would think a metal guitarist should do. It's important to me to be very honest in my approach to the guitar; let it flow from within rather than forcing anything. I love to improvise."

Jim Root 2009

"The first guitar I ever had was a right-handed Stratocaster turned upside down; the Jimi Hendrix cream color and stuff. I was never the biggest Hendrix fan, but I just loved his playing upside-down guitar and I just related. I've always related, and whether or not they're my favorite artists, you always have something in common with lefties. Kurt Cobain or Paul McCartney or Tim Armstrong from Rancid, or Ernie-C from Body Count."

Zacky Vengence 2005

209

210

"Throughout my guitar career, one of the things I thought was most important was to embrace constraints. Whether it's using only four little effects pedals or using the identical amplifier settings on my amp that I've used since 1988. And by embracing those limitations, the instrument then becomes your imagination. And you just don't run to the guitar store and try to buy that new piece of guitar gear and chase this, that, and the other. I've found an endless wellspring of inspiration in trying to think outside the box with a limited set of gear, rather than having an endless set of gear and not knowing what to do with it."

"Generally, I don't find guitar players particularly interesting, frankly. The influence and inspirations come from other sources than guitar playing. In the past, it's come from a pretty wide variety. I've tried to choose influences that were nonmusical to bring into my playing. Whether it would be a Malcolm X speech or a trip to the zoo or the sounds of the city or a horse race. The feelings you draw from different places, and just see where that takes your guitar playing as opposed to pentatonic this and that."

"Eddie Van Halen and Randy Rhoads were the ones I dedicated myself to as a young aspiring shredder."

"I like Steve Vai very much. I'm a big fan of his; I think he's great. One of my favorite guitar records is the Public Image record he played on; it's awesome. It's seeing him in that kind of context; I think it really throws him out of his normal element and pushed him. And the first David Lee Roth record, one of my favorites. Tasty."

Tom Morello 2005

"I'm not a master of even six strings, so when I actually went to seven, it was because I wanted that lower sound, that deeper tuning. That was what drove me into the seventh, and once I got comfortable playing the seven-string, my mentality has always been the same, even coming from the six-string. . . . As far as bringing in the eight-string, it's that same desire. I wanted that lower sound. I brought it out just to have fun. I didn't master the six-string; I certainly was not a master of the seven. If I could not master the six, then the eight is just a beast."

"I don't know theory, or haven't had any lessons growing up as a guitar player until recently. For me, the instrument has always just been a device and a tool to have fun with. My intent to take lessons is not to do anything else other than to learn some scales; to be able to switch modes and change the mood in the music."

Stephen Carpenter 2009

213

STEPHEN CARPENTER | 2000 ~ JAMES "MUNKY" SHAFFER AND BRIAN "HEAD" WELCH | 2000

"If it can be simple and powerful, then you've done it. If you do something complicated, it's a lot easier to sound impressive than being able to do something very simple. But there is a lot of complex stuff where it's like, 'Just shut up already!' And a lot of simple stuff where they think they're saying something and they're still saying nothing."

"As a player, I'm pretty much of a perfectionist. I love just locking in with rhythm sections and things like that because a lot of the funk element of what I did used to work that way."

Nuno Bettencourt 2002

"I just plug into an amp, I guess. I've never really analyzed it; I just know what sounds good to me. That's what I go for."

Rich Robinson 1999

"I'm a blues player, you know? I came from a modern-day blues kind of place. I was in so many different bands coming into this band: I was in one band that was progressive; I was in one band that was a funk group; I was in a modern-day blues band, and I was in a heavy metal band on Swan Song Records. So I had a couple of record deals before I got in this band. I was kind of like a very diverse player. But when I got in this band, we were touring with all these heavy metal acts, so I just pulled out my heavy metal chops. And that's the way I sounded, and as we started to mature and we started to find our stylistic voice as a band, I became more of a rock and roll player and I started to interject more of my blues chops into pop music. And that was my role, that's where I came in."

Richie Sambora 2004

216

217

"I think it's important to tell the younger people that music is a gift. When young guitarists develop that, you can actually heal people. With real music, you can make people cry and laugh and dance at the same time."

"Woodstock was magical. We flew in by helicopter, and backstage was like a disaster area. They told us we wouldn't go on until 6 or 8 o'clock at night, and we got there at 11 in the afternoon. I found Jerry Garcia and he had this great smile on his face, and the next thing I know, I've taken something, too. I thought by 8 p.m. I would come down; it wouldn't be a problem. Wrong! They told us we had to go on immediately or 'You don't play at all.' I said, 'Oh, God, just keep my guitar in tune and keep my fingers in the right place.' It was pretty dangerous."

"If you listen to John Lee Hooker moan, that's the tone I'm always trying to get. Jimi Hendrix's 'Voodoo Chile' are the types of low notes I want."

"Sonny Sharrock and Jeff Beck approach the guitar like a chainsaw massacre, but from that assault comes beautiful melodies. If I was going to tell Yngwie Malmsteen or Stevie Vai or Joe Satriani who to check out, I would tell them Sonny Sharrock. He is like the Sun Ra and 'Trane of the guitar. I told Jeff Beck about him and said, 'He's gonna scare the hell out of you.' He makes punk records sound like Donnie Osmond and Marie."

Carlos Santana 1994

220

"I'm first and foremost a rhythm guitar player; that's what I think of first. That syncopated, staccato, in-your-face, left and right, shotgun, two sides, double-barrel guitar thing. And whatever else goes with that as far as interweaving and throwing some other colors in there is fine."

"The better the guitar sound, the less notes you have to play. It's the sound between the notes that makes the solo really important and interesting."

Steve Stevens 1989

"One thing that afforded my guitar playing a rhythmatic sense was in the '80s a lot of guitar players worked with singers that had higher voices. Because Billy was sort of more in the Jim Morrison vein, my guitar took on a weight, because everything was kinda pitched lower, you know. So that if I was doing all this kinda high stuff, I mean, the majority of my rhythm stuff is based on the bottom three strings anyway you know, and uh, if you do a lot of this other stuff it becomes a little light. If you think about the Zeppelin riffs and stuff, all the great Zeppelin riffs are really based on those bottom three strings. And that allows you to orchestrate your guitar parts, to allow other parts to take their own place in the mix. There's only so much room available in a song sonically, and if you've got frequencies and parts that are fighting each other, you are going to end up with a very small-sounding song."

Steve Stevens 2008

222

BRAD GILLIS | 1985

"If you're going to play heavy metal, you have to have your own sound. You have to rise above the rest to have your own style and sound."

Brad Gillis 1984

"Most of my heroes were American Telly players; that whole trip: Robbie Robertson, Jesse Davis, James Burton, and Clarence White. All the sort of smart guys, the clever wise guy Telly players: Mike Bloomfield, Roy Buchanan, the list goes on and on."

———————

"My thing is the perfect tone—that perfect James Bond twang or power chord or electric sitar or that certain acoustic guitar feel. That to me was like getting my rocks off. Not a 20-minute guitar solo. I get bored listening to other people doing that."

———————

"I'm the Zelig of guitar players. I like the different idioms; I like being a chameleon and being able to adapt to different roles. It's great to do Cars records and then be able to do an R&B record with Peter Wolf and then do a rock and roll record. During the course of the day, I may listen from Eddie Lang and Joe Venuti to Joe Mavis and Merle Travis to Kraftwerk and King Crimson. I don't care as long as it's good."

Elliot Easton 1985

ELLIOT EASTON | 2006

224

225

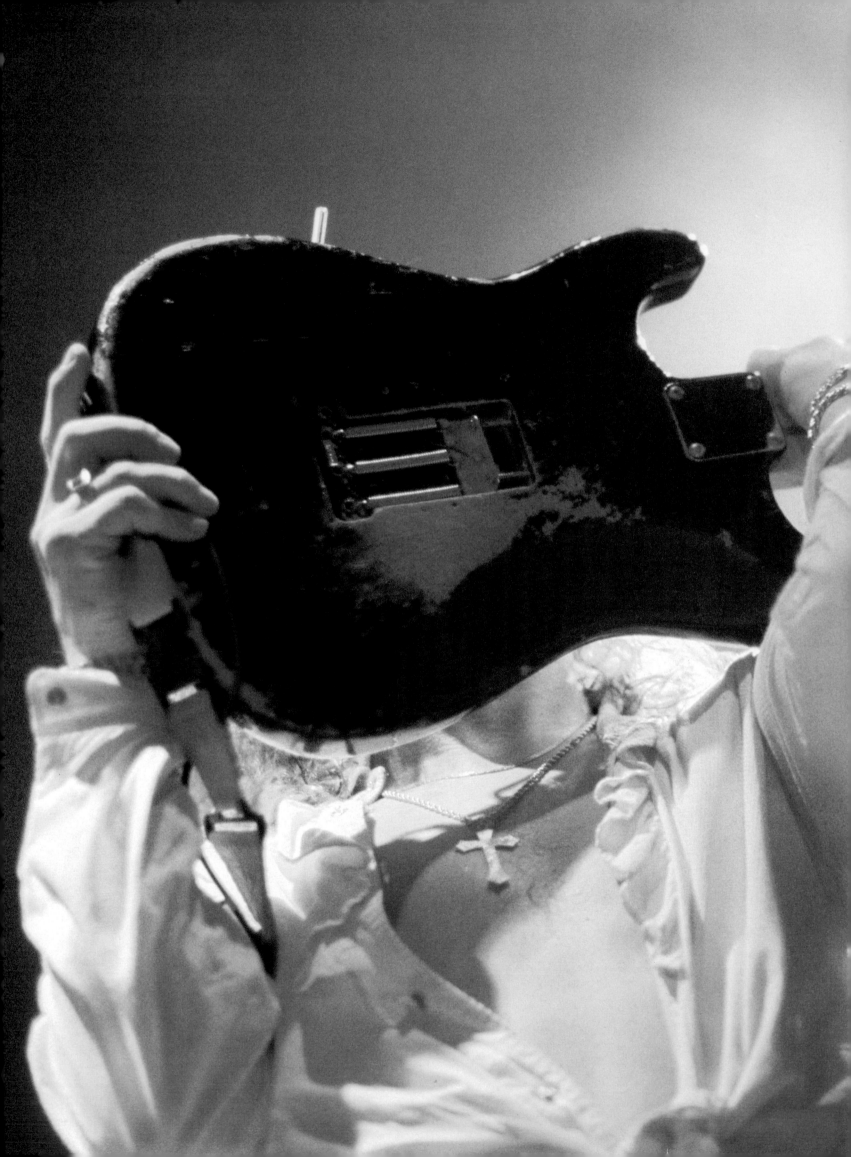

YNGWIE MALMSTEEN | 1986

"I think melody; I think song; I think vocals, arrangements . . . much, much, much before the guitar. The guitar comes in very long down the line. I want to have it where you can take the guitar player out and still have a good record. That's the way I want to look at it."

"It's a very funny thing when people ask me which bands I like, which guitar players. Which is a very old question but I seem to have to answer it anyway. The truth is, I don't very much care for guitar players, first of all. I never did. When I was very young, just a kid, I loved Ritchie Blackmore. I think I sort of faded away from that and got into classical music. There are loads of good guitar players, but they're still not my focal point. I wanted to do with the guitar what other people did with the violin or flute."

"There are only eight notes, and as far as I'm concerned, it's the attitude and the vibe. When I put solos on tape, I usually feel they suck. I usually throw it down and say, 'OK, let's do it one more time' or 'Fuck it, that's it.' That is the truth."

Yngwie Malmsteen 1995

230

"I'm more interested in melodic things. I think the biggest challenge when you go to play a solo is trying to invent a melody on the spot. I also think that a guitar player can only be as good as the band that's accompanying him. If the people backing you up are sensitive to what you're playing, you'll sound great; if they're just note-mashers, then you'll always sound mundane."

Frank Zappa 1977

"Once I get out onstage and turn my guitar on, it's a special thing to me—I love doing it. But I approach it more as a composer who happens to be able to operate an instrument called a guitar rather than 'Frank Zappa, Rock and Roll Guitar Hero.'"

"I'm not really a fast guitar player because I'm not picking everything I play. I only play fast when I think it's appropriate to the line I'm doing."

"There are a few guitar players that I've heard recently who I think are real good. I like Brian May of Queen; I think he's really excellent. And I always did like Wes Montgomery until they started smothering him with violins. I like Jeff, yeah. I've listened to *Wired*, and there are a couple of solos on there that I like. And I like some of his stuff on *Rough and Ready*. A person would be a moron not to appreciate McLaughlin's technique. The guy has certainly found out how to operate a guitar as if it were a machine gun."

Frank Zappa 1977

"The hardest thing for me to do is play straight up and down, absolutely the hardest thing to do. Stuff that everybody else does naturally just seems as impossible as shit to me. I don't think in little groups of two's and four's and stuff; they just don't come out that way. I can sit around and play five's and seven's all day long with no sweat. But the minute I've got to go *do-do-do-do/do-do-do-do*, it feels weird; it's like wearing tight shoes. So I'm going to keep practicing. It's like learning how to speak English—if you've been speaking something else all the time, it's like trying to develop a convincing English accent."

Frank Zappa circa early 1980s

FRANK ZAPPA | 1981

234

"Before I began to play the guitar, I would literally tremble with excitement inside whenever I would even see one, and the people who played them seemed like gods. I was never interested in its mechanics or history, but I was desperate to know everything I could about playing the guitar and creating those exotic sounds that could come out of it.

"As a teenager in the '70s, Page, Hendrix, Beck, and Brian May were my heroes. But I was always careful not to rehash their licks. That didn't make any sense to me. I couldn't do it anyway! I made conscious efforts to seek out melodies and techniques that I had not heard before. Once I found them, I would exaggerate them. I discovered that it's important to be able to identify what feels natural to you and cultivate it, regardless of what anyone else is doing.

"I would envision myself performing with command and control that looked effortless and elegant, using dynamics that ranged from extraordinarily subtle and tender to intensely brutal. In visualizing myself doing things that I couldn't do, before I knew it, I was doing them. I still do this. We become what we see ourselves as in our mind's eye.

"I have always felt that if you have good technique, it's easier to express your ideas with clarity and confidence, whether what you do is slow and melodic or frighteningly virtuosic. I wanted it all, but playing the guitar did not come naturally to me. I had to work hard at it, seemingly much harder than most.

"The look of written music on paper fascinated me, and I wanted to understand it inside and out. Luckily, that part of being a musician came very naturally to me. It's much easier to understand than you might think, but most people are either intimidated by it or just plain not interested. But it doesn't matter if you know music or not, because an effective player pools all his resources, whatever they are, to create his own unique expression. Yet the real effectiveness of what we do is based on our sincerity and confidence as we are doing it.

"Some play fast and inspired, and some are just fascinated watching their fingers meander. Some have no real technique but can make you weep. Some believe they are being minimal but soulful, but their playing is actually insipid. In the guitar universe, there's everything from Gandhi to gangbangers. You don't have to play fast to suck!

"Frankly, I have never thought I was ever quite good enough, or as good as I could be. I was in the habit of thinking that everyone was better than me. But I truly love the guitar and deeply enjoy the way I play. The 'laying of hands' on the instrument has always been, and always will be, a sacred privilege that I will never take for granted."

Steve Vai 2009

STEVE VAI | 2001

238

STEVE VAI | 2001 | 1987

"I think whatever guitar I pick up I can make sound a certain way. You should be able to pick up a guitar and make it sound like you."

"Right before I joined Lizzy, I bumped into Peter Green, who had left Fleetwood Mac. We admired each other's playing, and he said I could borrow his Les Paul. I couldn't believe it! I had it for a few days, and he called me up and said, 'What do you think of that guitar?' and he asked me if I wanted it. That was the guitar from *Hard Road* and all the Fleetwood Mac stuff. He told me to sell my guitar and whatever I got for mine, I could just give to him. Financially it was ludicrous because I didn't have a guitar that was worth anything like what his was worth. And I finally gave him about 100 pounds [approximately $250]."

Gary Moore 1984

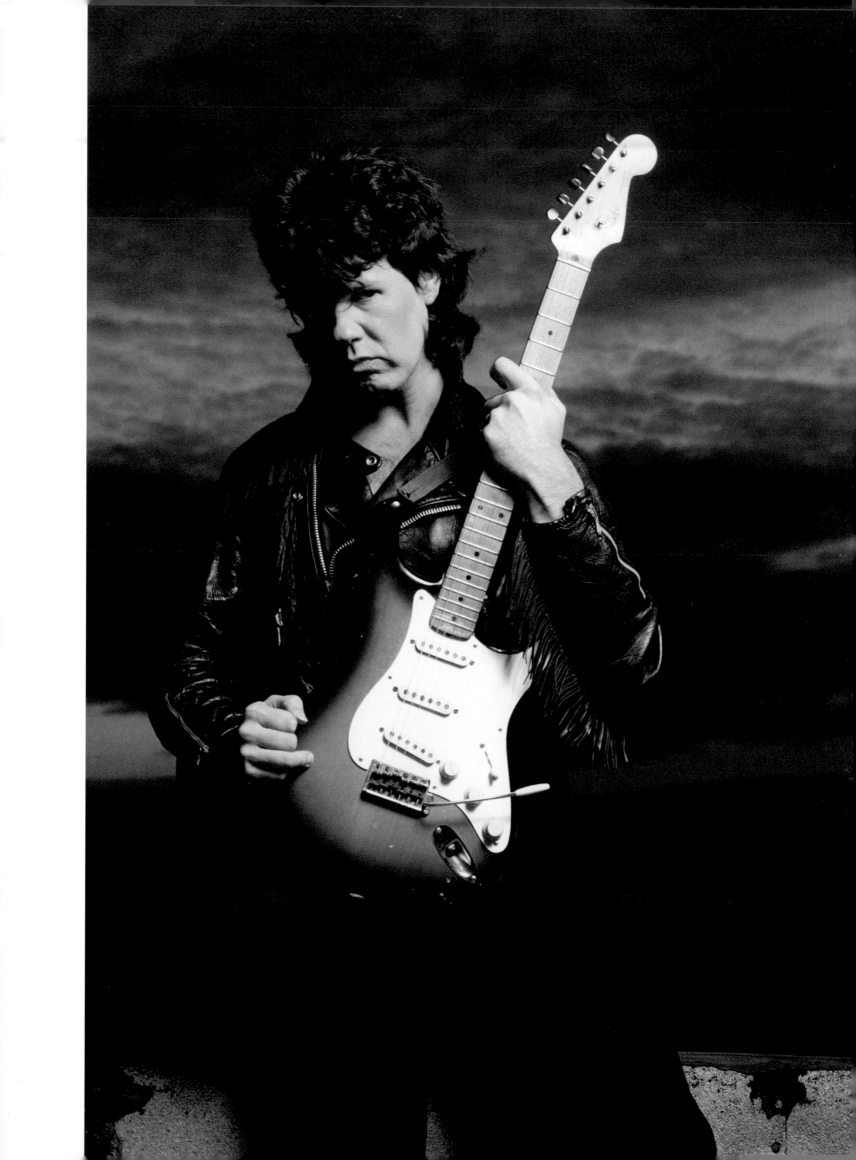

RANDY RHOADS | 1981

RANDY RHOADS | 1981

ZAKK WYLDE | 2004

"I always practice clean, but then I practice with distortion too because you have to learn how to control it. At the same time if you can play clean, it just makes it that much easier to play dirty."

―――――――――――――

"I think it's a copout when guys go, 'Ahh, he just fuckin' plays fast all the time.' It's like, 'Listen, you lazy motherfucker, if you fuckin' practice at all then maybe you'd be able to play fast.' Somebody like a real blues purist would say about Eddie Van Halen [that he] always plays fast. You can say B.B. King only plays three notes that are all he's ever played; he can't even play rhythm guitar and sing at the same time. And John McLaughlin only plays fast? John McLaughlin can play slow, too; listen to some of the records. Listen to Al Di Meola records, *Land of the Midnight Sun* and stuff like that. He does the melody, and when he wants to rip, he'll rip. If you can play fast, it just obviously shows you're dedicated to the instrument and you practice."

Zakk Wylde 2004

252

253

"It started with people like Randy Rhoads and Eddie Van Halen. It really started with Tony Iommi; that's the reason I wanted to play the guitar—because of Sabbath. Tony, and then obviously when Ozzy did the thing with Randy—and the first time I heard Eddie Van Halen it was like, 'Oh, my God!' After that it was hearing Yngwie and Al Di Meola and McLaughlin and *Friday Night in San Francisco: Live*. And then hearing Frank Marino and his live album. The first time I heard that thing it was, 'Holy shit.' Those were the guys who got me into the speed thing, and then hearing Albert Lee and even Alvin Lee, when I saw the Woodstock thing, 'I'm Going Home.' Back then there was hardly any distortion on his amp, and he was fuckin' shreddin'."

Zakk Wylde 2004

INDEX OF PHOTOGRAPHS